# Foundations
## for
# FAITH

Kenneth E. Hagin

17  16  15  14  13  12  11          15  14  13  12  11  10  09

*Foundations for Faith*
ISBN-13: 978-0-89276-067-1
ISBN-10: 0-89276-067-2

*In the U.S. write:*
Kenneth Hagin Ministries
P.O. Box 50126
Tulsa, OK 74150-0126
1-888-28-FAITH
www.rhema.org

*In Canada write:*
Kenneth Hagin Ministries
P.O. Box 335, Station D
Etobicoke (Toronto), Ontario
Canada, M9A 4X3
1-866-70-RHEMA
www.rhemacanada.org

# Contents

# How Do We Get Faith?

**Bible Texts:** Romans 10:8-10,13-14,17; Acts 11:13-14; 14:7-10; 8:5-8

**Central Truth:** God has provided the way whereby everyone can have faith.

We read in Hebrews 11:6, *"But without faith it is impossible to please him: for he that cometh to God must believe that he is, and that he is a rewarder of them that diligently seek him."*

If God demands we have faith when it is impossible for us to have faith, we have a right to challenge His justice. But if He places within our hands the means whereby faith can be produced, then the responsibility rests with us whether or not we have faith.

God has told us without faith it is impossible to please Him. But He also has told us how to get faith. If we don't have faith, it is not God's fault. To blame God for our lack of faith is nothing but ignorance. God has provided the way whereby everyone can have faith.

## Faith for Salvation

The Apostle Paul said we are saved by faith. *"For by grace are ye saved through faith; and that not of yourselves: it is the gift of God"* (Eph. 2:8). But how do you get faith to be saved?

**ROMANS 10:8-10,13-14,17**

**8 But what saith it? The word is nigh thee, even in thy mouth, and in thy heart: that is, the word of faith, which we preach;**

**9 That if thou shalt confess with thy mouth the Lord Jesus, and shalt believe in thine heart that God hath raised him from the dead, thou shalt be saved.**

**10 For with the heart man believeth unto righteousness; and with the mouth confession is made unto salvation. . . .**

**13 For whosoever shall call upon the name of the Lord shall be saved.**

**14** How then shall they call on him in whom they have not believed? and how shall they believe in him of whom they have not heard? and how shall they hear without a preacher? . . . **17** So then faith cometh by hearing, and hearing by the word of God.

After studying the passage of Scripture quoted above, what three steps does man take to receive salvation? (1. Confess 2. Believe 3. Accept.) To whom is this salvation available, according to verse 13? (Whosoever.) According to verse 17, where does faith come from? (By hearing the Word of God.)

**ACTS 11:13–14**

**13** And he shewed us how he [Cornelius] had seen an angel in his house, which stood and said unto him, Send men to Joppa, and call for Simon, whose surname is Peter; **14** Who shall tell thee words, whereby thou and all thy house shall be saved.

God instructed Cornelius to send for Peter in order to learn the plan of salvation. In the Great Commission, recorded in Mark 16:15–18, Jesus told His disciples, *"Go ye into all the world, and preach the gospel to every creature . . ."* Cornelius had not yet heard this glorious Gospel. He was not saved. God told Cornelius to send for Peter in order to learn the plan of salvation.

Why did Cornelius have to send for Peter? Why couldn't the angel have explained the plan of salvation to Cornelius just as well? (Angels cannot preach the Gospel. God has given this task to man.)

The verse *"Who shall tell thee words, whereby thou and all thy house shall be saved"* shows us that men are saved by hearing words! The reason for this is because *"faith cometh by hearing, and hearing by the word of God"* (Rom. 10:17).

## Faith for Healing

**ACTS 14:7–10**

**7** And there they [Paul and Barnabas] preached the gospel.
**8** And there sat a certain man at Lystra, impotent in his feet, being a cripple from his mother's womb, who never had walked.
**9** The same heard Paul speak: who stedfastly beholding him, and perceiving that he had faith to be healed,
**10** Said with a loud voice, Stand upright on thy feet. And he leaped and walked.

A casual reader of the Word once said concerning this passage of Scripture, "Isn't it wonderful how Paul healed that man?" However, Paul did not heal the man. The man was not healed because Paul was an apostle. He was not healed through Paul's faith. The man himself had the faith.

Paul did three things:

1. He preached the Gospel (v. 7).

2. He perceived that the man had faith to be healed (v. 9).
3. He told the man to stand up and walk (v. 10).

The man did three things:

1. He heard Paul preach (v. 9).
2. He had faith to be healed (v. 9).
3. He leaped and walked (v. 10).

The man was not healed by some power Paul had. The man himself had faith to be healed.

Where did the man get the faith to be healed? *By hearing Paul speak.* What did Paul speak? *He preached the Gospel.* Paul preached a Gospel of salvation and healing: *"For I am not ashamed of the gospel of Christ: for it is the power of God unto salvation to every one that believeth; to the Jew first, and also to the Greek"* (Rom. 1:16).

A footnote in the *Scofield Bible* referring to this verse says, "The Greek and Hebrew words for salvation imply the ideas of deliverance, safety, preservation, healing, and soundness." Therefore, Paul was saying, "I am not ashamed of the Gospel of Christ. It is the power of God unto deliverance, safety, preservation, healing, and soundness." Paul preached the *full* Gospel; not just part of it.

**ACTS 8:5–8**
**5 Then Philip went down to the city of Samaria, and preached Christ unto them.**

**6 And the people with one accord gave heed unto those things which Philip spake, hearing and seeing the miracles which he did.**
**7 For unclean spirits, crying with loud voice, came out of many that were possessed with them: and many taken with palsies, and that were lame, were healed.**
**8 And there was great joy in that city.**

The great miracles recorded in the above verses came about as the result of Philip's preaching Christ. The New Testament knows no Christ without Christ the Healer. Physical healing is part of the Gospel. If there is no Gospel of healing today, then neither is there a Gospel of salvation.

### Faith in Action

P.C. Nelson, who was for many years, a noted Baptist minister, said, "Healing is part and parcel of the Gospel." While pastoring a church in Detroit, Michigan, in 1921, he was struck by an automobile. The doctors said his left leg probably would have to be amputated. Even if they didn't have to take it off, it would be stiff.

As he lay in bed, the verses of Scripture in James 5:14–15 came to him: *"Is any sick, among you? let him call for the elders of the church; and let them pray over him, anointing him with oil in the name of the Lord: And the prayer of faith shall save the sick, and*

3

*the Lord shall raise him up; and if he have committed sins, they shall be forgiven him."*

Dr. Nelson tried to excuse himself to the Lord by saying that they didn't practice this in his church. The Lord reminded him that he had four Spirit-filled friends who believed in it, and He told Dr. Nelson to call them to come and pray for him. They came to his home, anointed him with oil, and prayed the prayer of faith for him. He was healed. His leg didn't have to be removed, and it was never stiff. *"Faith cometh by hearing, and hearing by the word of God."*

Many years ago, as a young Baptist boy, I lay on the bed of sickness. As I read Grandma Drake's "Methodist" Bible, I realized that I had never heard the *full* Gospel, just part of it. The more I read, the more I saw that I didn't have to die. The more I studied the Bible, the more I realized I could be healed!

The devil was right there, of course, bringing to my remembrance all the doubt and unbelief I had ever heard. He told me that healing had been done away with. Fortunately, I couldn't remember ever hearing that faith had been done away with. I also had to struggle with the teaching that God would heal *if* He wanted to. (This, however, was an even bigger insult to God than saying that He couldn't.)

I read in Mark 5:34 where Jesus spoke to the woman with the issue of blood, saying, *"Daughter, thy faith hath made thee whole; go in peace, and be whole of thy plague."* Jesus didn't say His power had made her whole; He said, "Daughter *THY FAITH hath made thee whole. . . ."* When I saw this, I knew then that, if *her* faith had made her whole, *my* faith could make me whole. And, thank God, it did.

My paralysis disappeared, my heart condition became normal, and I've been going at a hop, skip, and and jump ever since, preaching the Gospel in its fullness for more than 60 years.

---

**Memory Text:**
"So then faith cometh by hearing, and hearing by the word of God."
—Rom. 10:17

---

# What Is Faith?

**Bible Texts:** Hebrews 11:1; Mark 11:23-24; John 20:24-29; Romans 4:17-21

**Central Truth:** Faith is grasping the unrealities of hope and bringing them into the realm of reality.

A key verse in the study of faith is the familiar one found in Hebrews 11:1, *"Now faith is the substance of things hoped for, the evidence of things not seen."* Moffatt's translation of this verse reads, *"Now faith means that we are confident of what we hope for, convinced of what we do not see."*

Another translation says, "Faith is giving substance to things hoped for." Still another translation reads, "Faith is the warranty deed, the thing for which we have finally hoped is at last ours." Here God is telling us what faith is.

There are a number of kinds of faith. Everyone, saved and unsaved alike, has a natural, human faith. The above scripture, however, is talking about a supernatural faith—a faith that believes with the heart rather than believing what our physical senses may tell us. Faith, in other words, is grasping the unrealities of hope and bringing them into the realm of reality. And faith grows out of the Word of God.

Our text describes faith as *"the evidence of things not seen."* For example, you hope for finances to meet the obligations you have to pay. Faith gives the assurance that you will have the money when you need it. You hope for physical strength to do the work that you must do. Faith says, *"The Lord is the strength of my life; of whom shall I be afraid?"* (Ps. 27:1). Faith will say about itself everything that the Word says, for *faith in God is simply faith in His Word.*

I learned an important lesson in faith shortly after I was raised up from the bed of sickness many years ago. I needed work, and since this was during the Depression, work was not easy to find. I was able to get a job in a nursery helping pull up peach trees. With another boy on the other side of the tree, together we would pull up these two-year-old trees to fill orders that had come in. This was really hard work—especially since I had been bedfast for 16 months and at this time had been up only a few months.

Each day the number of workers would be fewer and fewer, and each day someone would say to me, "Well, I didn't think you'd make it to today. You know, two or three quit yesterday."

"If it weren't for the Lord I wouldn't be here," I would answer. "You see, His strength is my strength. The Bible says, *The Lord is the strength of my life . . .'* My life consists of the physical as well as the spiritual, and the Lord is the strength of my life."

If I had gone according to my feelings, I wouldn't have gotten out of bed. I acted on the Word because I knew what faith was. I never received any strength until I started to work.

Many people want to receive and then believe they've got it. It doesn't work that way, though. You have to believe first, and then you will receive.

So I would pull myself out of bed each morning and go to work, gaining strength as I went along, trusting in God's Word. Although I was the weakest and skinniest one among that group of men, I was the last one to stay on the job.

We may *say* we know God's Word is good, but we will never really *know*

until we have acted on it and have reaped its results. Faith is giving substance to things hoped for.

I went to work. I acted on God's Word. I hoped for physical strength to do the work I knew must be done, and as I acted on God's Word, my faith gave substance to that which I hoped for. Hope says, "I'll have it *sometime*." Faith says, "I have it *now*."

## Head Faith vs. Heart Faith

John Wesley once said that the devil has given the Church a substitute for faith; one that looks and sounds so much like faith that few people can tell the difference. This substitute he called "mental assent." Many people read God's Word and agree that it is true, but they are agreeing only with their minds. And that is not what gets the job done. It is heart faith that receives from God.

MARK 11:23–24
**23 For verily I say unto you, That whosoever shall say unto this mountain, Be thou removed, and be thou cast into the sea; and shall not doubt in his heart, but shall believe that those things which he saith shall come to pass; he shall have whatsoever he saith.**
**24 Therefore I say unto you, What things soever ye desire, when ye pray, believe that ye receive them, and ye shall have them.**

How can we tell whether we have this heart faith or we are just mentally agreeing? Mental assent says, "I know God's Word is true. I know God has promised healing, but for some reason I can't get it; I can't understand it." However, real faith in God's Word says, "If God's Word says it's so, then it's so. It is mine. I have it now. I have it even though I can't see it."

I've heard people say, "But the thing I have been praying about hasn't come to pass yet." If you already had it, you wouldn't have to believe it, for then you would know it. You have to take that step of *believing* in order to come to the place of *knowing.* Too many people want to know it from the standpoint of its coming to pass, and then believe it. We must believe it because God's Word *says* it is ours. *Then* it materializes.

Notice from Mark 11:24 that the receiving comes *after* the believing:

*"What things soever ye desire, when ye pray, believe that ye receive them, and ye shall have them."* Jesus was simply saying, "You've got to believe you have it before you can receive it."

I never have been able to receive physical healing for myself without first believing I have it. Every symptom in my body cries out, "You don't have it." I simply stand firm on what God's Word says about my healing and continue to claim that I am healed. Results are then forthcoming. But if I were to sit around, groan and sigh, gripe, and complain, waiting until every symptom was gone and any feelings corresponded with my

faith before I believed, I never would get very far, because *"faith is . . . the evidence of things not seen."*

## Thomas' Faith vs. Abraham's Faith

Too many Christians have a "Thomas faith" when they should have an "Abraham faith." Thomas said, "I'll not believe until I can see Him," whereas "Abraham staggered not at the promise of God . . . but was strong in faith."

### JOHN 20:24–29

**24 But Thomas, one of the twelve, called Didymus, was not with them when Jesus came.**

**25 The other disciples therefore said unto him, We have seen the Lord. But he said unto them, Except I shall see in his hands the print of the nails, and put my finger into the print of the nails, and thrust my hand into his side, I will not believe.**

**26 And after eight days again his disciples were within, and Thomas with them: then came Jesus, the doors being shut, and stood in the midst, and said, Peace be unto you.**

**27 Then saith he to Thomas, Reach hither thy finger, and behold my hands; and reach hither thy hand, and thrust it into my side: and be not faithless, but believing.**

**28 And Thomas answered and said unto him, My Lord and my God.**

**29 Jesus saith unto him, Thomas, because thou hast seen me, thou hast**

believed: blessed are they that have not seen, and yet have believed.

Why did Thomas find it hard to believe Jesus was alive? Thomas knew of the nails that pierced Jesus' hands and the spear that was thrust into His side. His physical senses told him Jesus was dead. Thomas was using head knowledge, rather than heart faith.

Compare now the faith of Abraham:

**ROMANS 4:17–21**
**17 (As it is written, I have made thee [Abraham] a father of many nations,) before him whom he believed, even God, who quickeneth the dead, and calleth those things which be not as though they were.**
**18 Who against hope believed in hope, that he might become the father of many nations, according to that which was spoken, So shall thy seed be.**
**19 And being not weak in faith, he considered not his own body now dead, when he was about an hundred years old, neither yet the deadness of Sarah's womb:**
**20 He staggered not at the promise of God through unbelief; but was strong in faith, giving glory to God;**
**21 And being fully persuaded that, what he had promised, he was able also to perform.**

Notice the difference in Thomas' faith and Abraham's faith. Thomas had only a natural, human faith which said, "I'm not going to believe unless I can see and feel." Abraham, however, believed God's Word, considering not his own body—his own natural senses. If Abraham didn't consider physical knowledge or feelings, what did he consider? (The Word of God.)

Years ago when I was healed of heart trouble, I was struggling along some of these faith lines that many people do. Alarming heart symptoms would return.

While praying and standing on the promises of God, even while suffering severe pain, the Lord reminded me of Abraham, who *"considered not his own body."* He showed me I should not consider my body, but rather I should consider His Word. As I did this, repeating to myself some of God's promises in the Scriptures regarding healing, such as, *"Himself took our infirmities, and bare our sicknesses,"* every symptom would leave. Too many times we focus our attention on the wrong thing. We consider our physical body and the symptoms rather than looking to God's Word.

In one church I visited, a certain woman regularly ended her testimony with, "You pray for me. I believe I've got cancer." No doubt if she keeps believing it, she will get it. (Jesus said, *"According to your faith be it unto you."*) Another person requested prayer, saying, "Please pray for me. I believe I'm taking a cold." If that is the way you believe, it won't do any good for me to pray, because *"According to your faith be it unto you"* (Matt. 9:29). We need to walk by faith, not by sight.

Some have misunderstood this type of teaching, thinking I tell people to deny all symptoms and go on as if they weren't even there. They think I am teaching Christian Science. However, this is not Christian Science; this is Christian *sense*. We do not deny pains and other symptoms, for they are very real. Instead, we look beyond them to God's promises.

Real faith in the Word says, "If God says it is so, it is so. If He says, *'By whose stripes ye were healed,'* I am healed. If He says, *'My God shall supply all your need,'* He does. If He says, *'The Lord is the strength of my life,'* He is." In other words, real faith simply says about one's self what the Word says.

Real faith is built on the Word. We should meditate on the Word, dig deeply into it, and feed upon it. Then the Word becomes a part of us, just as natural food becomes a part of our physical body when we eat. What natural food is to the physical man, the Word of God is to the spiritual man. The Word builds confidence and assurance into us.

**Memory Text:**
"Now faith is the substance of things hoped for, the evidence of things not seen."
—Heb. 11:1

# Faith vs. Hope

**Bible Texts:** 1 Corinthians 13:13; Ephesians 2:8-9; Romans 10:9-10,13

**Central Truth:** It takes a positive faith—a now faith—to get positive results.

When Paul, writing to the Corinthians, said, *"And now abideth faith, hope, charity, these three; but the greatest of these is charity"* (1 Cor. 13:13), he was not inferring that hope and faith are not important.

Each has its place, and one cannot be substituted for another. We cannot substitute love for hope. Neither can we substitute hope for faith. Yet so many people try to receive things from God on the basis of hope rather than faith.

### Faith Is Now

*Hope looks to the future.* It is always future tense. *Faith is now.* Faith says, "I'll receive the answer right now. I have it now." It is not hoping that gets the job done; it is believing.

Someone said, "Well, I believe I will receive my healing—sometime." That's not faith, that's hope, because it is looking to some indefinite, future time. Faith says, "I receive my healing—now!"

In one modern translation of the New Testament, the familiar verse in Hebrews 11:1 reads, "Faith is giving substance . . . to things hoped for."

If you need healing, you don't want it in the future; you want it right now, especially if you're in pain. If you are seeking the baptism of the Holy Spirit, you want to receive now, not at some indefinite future time. If you need salvation, you cannot put it off to the future, for that may be too late.

I have talked to people who told me they *hoped* to be saved. Some of them are now dead. They left the world unsaved, because salvation that is based on hope never comes to fruition.

**EPHESIANS 2:8–9**

**8 For by grace are ye saved through faith; and that not of yourselves: it is the gift of God:**

**9 Not of works, lest any man should boast.**

**ROMANS 10:9–10,13**

**9 That if thou shalt confess with thy mouth the Lord Jesus, and shalt believe in thine heart that God hath raised him from the dead, thou shalt be saved.**

**10 For with the heart man believeth unto righteousness; and with the mouth confession is made unto salvation . . .**

**13 For whosoever shall call upon the name of the Lord shall be saved.**

The above verses point man to the plan of salvation. We see that it is by faith—not hope—that we are saved. Jesus promised He will not cast any out who come to Him, but will save all who *"call upon the name of the Lord."* Therefore, we don't need to hope that He will save us. He said He would.

### How Do We Get Faith?

Faith, we know, grows out of the Word of God. *"So then faith cometh by hearing, and hearing by the word of God"* (Rom. 10:17). Another translation of this verse reads, "Faith is the warranty deed, that the thing for which you have fondly hoped is at last yours."

Faith is *"the evidence of things not seen,"* as we read in Hebrews 11:1. To illustrate, you might hope for finances to meet a certain obligation, but faith gives you the assurance that you will have the money when you need it. You might hope for physical strength to do a job you must do, but faith says, *"The Lord is the strength of my life"* (Ps. 27:1). In other words, faith says the same thing the Word of God says.

Unbelief is really taking sides against God's Word. There are those who talk unbelief and take sides *against* the Word of God, and then wonder why God's Word doesn't work for them. *If we want God's Word to work for us, we must agree with it.*

Many times when I ask people who come for prayer in my meetings if they believe they will be healed, they answer, "Well, I sure *hope* I will." I tell them they won't, because we receive from God by faith, not hope. Still others answer, "Well, I want to." But I tell them, "You might want a new Cadillac, but that doesn't mean you'll get one. You see, just wanting to won't get the job done."

It's not hoping or wanting: It's faith that gets the job done. You will not receive from God because you hope. Nowhere does the Bible say that when we pray, we shall receive what we hope for. God's Word does say, however, ". . . *What things soever ye desire, when ye pray, BELIEVE that ye receive them, and ye shall have them"* (Mark 11:24). Jesus also said, *"And all things, whatsoever ye shall ask in prayer, BELIEVING, ye shall receive"* (Matt. 21:22). Not hoping, but believing.

Notice in the definition of faith in Hebrews 11:1 ("Now faith is the substance of things hoped for, the evidence of things not seen"), the verb "is" is in the present tense. Remember, if it's not now, it's not faith. Faith is present tense; hope is future tense. Even though you might say you believe, if you are putting it into the future, you are not believing; you're hoping. In order for it to work, it must be in the correct tense—the present tense. Some people always are believing that God is *going* to do something for them, but faith believes that He *has done*, and *is doing*.

Some years ago while I was preaching in Oklahoma, a woman who hadn't taken a step in four years was brought to the service for prayer. She was in her seventies, and the doctors had said she never would walk again. At the close of the service when we were ready to have prayer for the sick, her friends brought her forward and sat her down on the altar.

I knelt in front of her, laid my hands on her, and prayed. Then I said, "Now arise and walk in the Name of the Lord Jesus Christ."

She did her best to get up, but all the time she was crying and praying, "O dear Jesus, please heal me. Please let me walk. Oh, please . . . please!" She continued in this vein for some time until finally I was able to quiet her enough to talk to her. I asked her, "Sister, did you know that you are healed?"

Astonished, she looked up at me and said, "Oh, am I?"

"Yes," I said, "you are healed, and I will prove it to you from the Bible." Then I opened my Bible to First Peter 2:24, handed it to her, and asked her to read the verse aloud.

She read, *"Who his own self bare our sins in his own body on the tree, that we, being dead to sins, should live unto righteousness: by whose stripes ye were healed."* I asked her to repeat the last phrase, and she read, " . . . *by whose stripes ye were healed."*

Then I asked her the question, "Is 'were' past tense, future tense, or present tense?"

"It is past tense," she answered.

"If you *were* healed by Jesus' stripes, then you *are* healed now, aren't you?" I said. A smile spread across her face and her eyes lit up with new understanding. Then I told her, "Just lift your hands and look up to Him. Begin to praise Him because you *are* healed, present tense. Because you *are* healed—not going to be—you *are* . . . now."

With childlike faith she looked up and said, "Dear Lord Jesus, I'm so glad I'm healed." She hadn't walked a step and therefore had no physical evidence of healing whatever. Yet she said, "I'm so glad I'm healed."

I turned to her and said, "Now, my sister, arise and walk in Jesus' Name." Immediately she jumped off that altar like a 16 year old, and walked, leaped, ran, and praised God.

You see, we had to help her get it in the right tense—because faith is present tense. As long as we are struggling to receive, hoping to see the answer sometime, it won't work. That is just hope. Faith says, " It's mine. I have it now."

Hope, of course, used properly is most blessed and beautiful. We have a blessed hope in the soon return of our Lord Jesus Christ, the Resurrection of the righteous dead, the Rapture of the living saints, the hope of heaven, and the hope of seeing our loved ones and friends. We thank God for that hope. But this is all future tense.

Jesus is coming, whether we believe It or not. He is coming because the Word says so. The Resurrection will take place whether we have faith or not. The dead in Christ will rise to meet Him in the air, whether we believe or not. Our faith, or lack of faith, will not affect these events. Jesus is coming back again, because the Word says He will. This is the blessed hope all Christians look forward to.

But it is faith, not hope, that can change the impossible to the possible. It is faith, not hope, that brings healing and victory.

Hope is a good waiter, but a poor receiver. Too many times I've heard people say, "I'm hoping and praying," or "All we can do now is hope and pray." If that is all you are doing, you're defeated. It takes a positive faith—a *now* faith—to get positive results.

---

**Memory Text:**
"And now abideth faith, hope, charity, these three; but the greatest of these is charity."
—1 Cor. 13:13

---

# Faith Sees the Answer

**Bible Texts:** Proverbs 4:20-22; Hebrews 13:5-6; 4:14; Mark 11:23

**Central Truth:** By continually looking at the Word, faith sees the answer.

In our past lessons, we have learned that faith is not something we have as much as it is something we do. We have seen that faith is not *hoping* that we will see the answer in the *future*; faith is *believing* that we have the answer *now*. The eyes of faith see the answer as having already happened.

**PROVERBS 4:20–22**

**20 My son, attend to my words; incline thine ear unto my sayings.**

**21 Let them not depart from thine eyes; keep them in the midst of thine heart.**

**22 For they** [my words] **are life unto those that find them, and health to all their flesh.**

Notice that this scripture says, *"Let them* [my words] *not depart from thine eyes. . . ."* Many people fail because they see themselves as failing.

If they are sick, they think of themselves as dying.

God's Word says, *"Himself* [Jesus] *took our infirmities, and bare our sicknesses"* (Matt. 8:17). If that Word does not depart from before your eyes, you are bound to see yourself without sickness and without disease. You will see yourself as well.

If, however, you do not see yourself as without sickness, then that Word has departed from before your eyes. And even though God wants to make health a reality in your life, He cannot, because you are not acting on His Word.

Notice also the 22nd verse, *"For they* [my words] *are life unto those that find them, and health to all their flesh."* The Hebrew word translated "health" here is also the word for medicine. In other words, "My words, are medicine to all their flesh."

The first two verses of this passage tell us the directions for taking this medicine. What are these directions? ("Attend to," or study God's Word, and "keep them in the midst of thine heart," or obey this Word.)

And what is God's medicine? "My words are life unto those that find them, and medicine to all their flesh." But the medicine has to be taken according to directions in order to work. And one of the directions is, *"Let them* [my words] *not depart from thine eyes."* Keep looking at what the Word says.

Too many people pray and pray, but they never see themselves with the answer. They just see everything getting worse. They keep looking at the wrong thing—at the symptoms, at conditions, at themselves—and so they walk in unbelief and destroy the effects of their praying.

Get your mind on the answer. See yourself as having received. Constantly affirm, even in the face of contradictory evidence, that God has heard your prayer because the Word says so. That's when you'll get results.

You have to believe you've got it before you can receive it. *"What things soever ye desire, when ye pray, believe that ye receive them, and ye shall have them"* (Mark 11:24). The believing comes *before* the receiving.

There are those who say, "I'm not going to believe anything I can't see." But in the natural we believe a lot of things we can't see. The whole world became alarmed when atomic bombs were being exploded, releasing radioactive material into the atmosphere. You can't see it or feel it, but it is a destructive power nevertheless.

## Faith Contradicts Circumstances

HEBREWS 13:5–6

5 . . . for he hath said, I will never leave thee, nor forsake thee.
6 So that we may boldly say, The Lord is my helper, and I will not fear what man shall do unto me.

Are we boldly saying that the Lord is our Helper? That is what we should be saying.

"Well, you all pray for me, I feel as if the Lord has forsaken me," cried one poor sister. "I don't know if I can make it or not. I hope I can. Pray for me that I'll hold out faithful to the end." This is a familiar request in prayer and testimony meetings. But that is not what God told us to say!

Too many people are boldly saying, "I'm whipped, I'm defeated. The devil's got me bound." But nowhere in the Bible do we find where God said to boldly say that.

God said, *"I will never leave thee, nor forsake thee."* So that we may boldly say, *"The Lord is my helper."*

Let's quit saying the wrong thing and start saying the right thing. Say the

Lord is your Helper. Say that the Lord is your Healer. Say that the Lord took your infirmities and bore your sicknesses. Keep talking about the right thing. Keep believing the right thing.

Wrong thinking, wrong believing, and wrong talking will defeat you. The devil can't defeat you, because Jesus already has defeated the devil *for* you. Satan doesn't defeat you; you defeat yourself. Or if he does, you permit him to do so. It is a consent of ignorance.

God has given us His Word to direct us so our believing will be right. If our thinking is right and our believing is right, our talking will be right. "The Lord is my helper." "The Lord is my strength."

## Faith 'Says' the Answer

Real faith in the Word says that if God says it is so, it's so. If He says *". . . by whose stripes ye were healed"* (1 Peter 2:24), we are healed. If He says, *"My God shall supply all your need according to his riches in glory by Christ Jesus"* (Phil. 4:19), He does it. If the Word says, *". . . the Lord is the strength of my life"* (Ps. 27:1), He is.

In other words, real faith in God simply says about one's self what the Word says. We have what the Word says we have. We are what the Word says we are. If God says we are strong, we are. If He says we are healed, we are. If He says He cares for me, He does.

**HEBREWS 4:14**

**14 Seeing then that we have a great high priest, that is passed into the heavens, Jesus the Son of God, let us hold fast our profession.**

Because Jesus is our High priest and sits at the right hand of God in heaven, making intercession for us, we can have the answers to our petitions now. Looking up the Greek word translated "profession," I learned that it should read, "Let us hold fast to saying the same things."

Jesus is in heaven, representing us at the throne of God. He is saying "I took their place, I died for them as their Substitute." Jesus didn't die for Himself. He didn't need to redeem Himself, because He wasn't lost. He died for us. He became our Substitute. He took our sins. He bore our sicknesses and carried our diseases. He died for us, arose from the dead for us, and ascended on high for us. He is up there now saying, "I did that for them," and we are to hold fast to saying the same things down here.

**MARK 11:23**

**23 . . . whosoever shall say unto this mountain, Be thou removed, and be thou cast into the sea; and shall not doubt in his heart, but shall believe that those things which he saith shall come to pass; he shall have whatsoever he saith.**

It isn't just a matter of faith going out of your heart toward God without your saying anything. That won't work. Nowhere in the Bible do we read that we should do that.

Faith *kept only in your heart* never will bring healing to your body, the infilling of the Holy Spirit, or an answer to prayer. But faith in your heart *released through your lips* will bring results.

---

### Memory Text:
"Let them [my words] not depart from thine eyes . . ."
—Prov. 4:21

---

# Faith vs. Feelings

**Bible Texts:** John 20:24–29; 2 Corinthians 5:17

**Central Truth:** A formula for faith is:
(1) Find a promise in God's Word
for whatever you are seeking.
(2) Believe God's Word.
(3) Do not consider contradictory
circumstances.
(4) Praise God for the answer.

The beloved man of faith Smith Wigglesworth once said, "I can't understand God by feelings. I can't understand the Lord Jesus Christ by feelings. I can only understand God the Father and Jesus Christ by what the Word says about them. God is everything the Word Says He is. We need to get acquainted with Him through the Word."

Too many people try to get acquainted with God through their feelings. When they feel good, they think God has heard their prayers. When they don't feel particularly good, they think He has not heard them. Their faith is based on their feelings, whereas it should be based on God's Word.

## A 'Thomas' Faith

**JOHN 20:24–29**

**24** But Thomas, one of the twelve, called Didymus, was not with them when Jesus came.

**25** The other disciples therefore said unto him, We have seen the Lord. But he said unto them, Except I shall see in his hands the print of the nails, and put my finger into the print of the nails, and thrust my hand into his side, I will not believe.

**26** And after eight days again his disciples were within, and Thomas with them: then came Jesus, the doors being shut, and stood in the midst, and said, Peace be unto you.

**27** Then saith he to Thomas, Reach hither thy finger, and behold my hands; and reach hither thy hand, and thrust it into my side: and be not faithless, but believing.

28 And Thomas answered and said unto him, My Lord and my God.

29 Jesus saith unto him, Thomas, because thou hast seen me, thou hast believed: blessed are they that have not seen, and yet have believed.

Thomas was one who based his faith upon his feelings. He said he would not believe unless he could *see* with his own eyes the prints of the nails in Jesus' hands, and *touch* these nail-prints with his own hands. He relied on what he could see and touch, not on what God had to say.

We have many "Thomas Christians" today—those who believe only what they can feel, see, hear, or touch. Real faith in God is based upon the Word of God. Real faith says, "If God says it is true, it is." Believing God is believing His Word. If God's Word says He hears me, I know He hears me, because His Word cannot lie.

If our faith is based upon feelings, we are just using natural human faith, and we cannot get spiritual results with natural human faith. We have to use scriptural faith—Bible faith—believing in God's Word.

Once I prayed for a woman who had been through many healing lines, but she never had received her healing. After I prayed, she immediately said, "I haven't got it yet. Pray again." I prayed

again, and when I was finished, she said the same thing

After praying a third time with seemingly no results I asked her, "When are you going to start believing you are healed?"

"Well," she said, "when I get healed."

"What in the world would you want to believe it for, then? It seems to me that you would know it then," I told her.

Anyone can believe what he can feel, hear, or see. We live and operate in the physical realm most of the time, and obviously we have to walk by sight *then*. But when it comes to Bible things—to spiritual things—we don't walk by sight; we walk by faith.

## Healing Is Spiritual

God's healing is spiritual healing. If medical science heals, it heals through the physical. Christian Science heals through the mind. But when God heals, He heals through the spirit.

**2 CORINTHIANS 5:17**
17 Therefore if any man be in Christ, he is a new creature: old things are passed away; behold, all things are become new.

Spiritual healing, or divine healing, is received from God in the same way that the New Birth, which is a rebirth of the spirit, is received.

When you are born again, it is not your body that is born again, because you still have the same body you always had. When Paul said, *"Therefore if any man be in Christ, he is a new creature . . . ,"* he was not talking about man's body being made new. The New Birth doesn't change the physical in any way. After you are saved, the man on the inside is to dominate the physical, of course, but it is this inner man who is born again.

The New Birth is the rebirth of the human spirit. Jesus said, *"That which is born of the flesh is flesh; and that which is born of the Spirit is spirit"* (John 3:6). We cannot tell immediately just what has happened on the inside of a person, because it takes place in the human spirit. But if a person walks in the light of what he has, in the process of time it will become obvious.

We often were mistaken when we saw people come to the altar, pray, cry, jump up, and hug everyone, acting so happy. Then they were never seen again. We really thought they had received something marvelous from God, but it was just an emotional experience, not the New Birth.

At other times we saw people come to the altar for salvation who were not emotional at all. We wondered if they had received anything from the Lord. We thought they were not at the altar long enough for anything. Yet many of these became outstanding Christians during their lifetimes. (This is another example of faith based on physical senses.)

I certainly believe in feeling, but I put it last. God's Word comes first, faith in God's Word second, and feeling last. Too many people turn it around and put feeling first, faith in their feelings second, and the Word of God last. These people never will make a success of anything.

Walking in the natural, we do have to go by our physical senses. (For example, if we are crossing a street and our eyes tell us cars are coming, we must wait until they pass.) But too many people try to believe in God with that physical, natural faith, and if their physical senses tell them it's not so, they believe it's not so. Our physical senses have nothing to do with the Bible. God's Word is true, regardless of our feelings or the circumstances: *"For ever, O Lord, thy word is settled in heaven"* (Ps. 119:89).

## Formula for Faith

Here is a formula for faith that you can make work for you:

*First,* have God's Word for whatever you may be seeking; *second,* believe God's Word; *third,* refuse to consider the contradictory circumstances, or what your physical senses may tell you about it; and, *fourth,* give praise to God for the answer.

Follow these four steps, and you always will get results. These are four certain steps to deliverance, healing, answered prayer, or whatever you may be seeking from the Lord.

---

### Memory Text:
"For ever, O Lord, thy word is settled in heaven."

—Ps. 119:89

---

# What It Means to Believe With the Heart
## (Part 1)

**Bible Texts:** 1 Thessalonians 5:23; Romans 12:1-2; Luke 16:19-25

**Central Truth:** Man is a spirit; he has a soul; and he lives in a body.

For years I searched for a satisfactory explanation of what it means to believe with the heart. I read Mark 11:23, which says, *"For verily I say unto you, That whosoever shall say unto this mountain, Be thou removed, and be thou cast into the sea; and shall not doubt in HIS HEART, but shall believe that those things which he saith shall come to pass; he shall have whatsoever he saith."*

Romans 10:10 also talks about believing with the heart: *"For WITH THE HEART man believeth unto righteousness. . . . "*

The word "heart" used in these scriptures does not refer to the physical organ that pumps blood through our body and keeps us alive. That would be believing God with our body. We couldn't believe with our physical heart any more than we could believe with our physical hand or finger. The word "heart" is used to convey a thought.

Notice how we use the word "heart" today. When we talk about the heart of a tree, we mean the center, the very core. When we talk about the heart of a subject, we mean the most important part of that subject, the very center of it, the main part around which the rest revolves. And when God speaks of man's heart, He is speaking about the main part of man, the very center of his being, which is the spirit.

### Man Is a Spirit

**1 THESSALONIANS 5:23**
**23 And the very God of peace sanctify you wholly; and I pray God your whole SPIRIT and SOUL and BODY be preserved blameless unto the coming of our Lord Jesus Christ.**

The terms "spirit of man" and "heart of man" are used interchangeably throughout the Bible. We know that man is a spirit, because he is made in the image and likeness of God, and Jesus said, *"God is a Spirit . . ."* (John 4:24).

Thus, it is not our physical bodies that are like God, for the Bible says that God is not a man. Remember, there is an inward man and an outward man. Man is a *spirit*; he has a *soul*, and he lives in a *body*.

Paul said in his letter to the Romans, *"For he is not a Jew, which is one outwardly; neither is that circumcision, which is outward in the flesh: But he is a Jew, which is one inwardly, and CIRCUMCISION IS THAT OF THE HEART, IN THE SPIRIT, and not in the letter; whose praise is not of men, but of God"* (Rom. 2:28–29). According to this text, the heart is the spirit.

Speaking to Nicodemus, Jesus said, *"Ye must be born again"* (John 3:7). Nicodemus, being human, could think only in the natural; therefore, he asked, *"How can a man be born when he is old? can he enter the second time into his mother's womb, and be born?"* (v. 4). Jesus answered, *"That which is born of the flesh is flesh, and that which is born of the Spirit is spirit"* (v. 6). The New Birth is a rebirth of the human spirit.

In John's Gospel we also read where Jesus told the woman at the well in Samaria, *"God is a Spirit: and they that worship him must worship him in spirit and in truth"* (John 4:24). We cannot contact God with our body or with our mind. We can contact God with our spirit.

First Corinthians 14:14 says, *"For if I pray in an unknown tongue, my spirit prayeth, but my understanding is unfruitful."* The spirit is not the mind. Some people mistakenly think that the mind is the spirit. However, as this verse indicates, we know that when we speak in tongues, this does not come from our mind, or our own human thinking, but from our spirit— from our innermost being—from the Holy Spirit within our spirit. Paul went on to say, *"What is it then? I will pray with the spirit, and I will pray with the understanding also . . ."* (v. 15). In other words, Paul was saying that his spirit is the real Paul.

## The Inward Man

Paul also said, *"For which cause we faint not; but though our outward man perish, yet the inward man is renewed day by day"* (2 Cor. 4:16). Paul pointed out that there is an outward man and an inward man. The outward man is the body. The inward man is the spirit. And the spirit has a soul.

In First Corinthians 9:27 Paul said, *"But I keep under my body, and bring it into subjection: lest that by any means, when I have preached to others, I myself should be a castaway."* If the body were the real man, Paul would have said, "I keep myself under; I bring myself into subjection." He refers to the body as "it." "I" is the man on the inside, the inward man who has been reborn. We do something with our body: We bring it into subjection. The man we look at is not the real man; it is just the house we live in.

We can now more easily understand Paul's writings to the saints at Rome:

**ROMANS 12:1–2**
**1  I beseech you therefore, brethren, by the mercies of God, that ye present your bodies a living sacrifice, holy, acceptable unto God, which is your reasonable service.**
**2  And be not conformed to this world: but be ye transformed by the renewing of your mind, that ye may prove what is that good, and acceptable, and perfect, will of God.**

In this epistle, Paul was not writing to unbelievers, but to Christians. He addresses his letter *"To all that be in Rome, beloved of God, called to be saints..."* (Rom. 1:7). Although he was writing to men and women who had been born again, he said they needed to do something with their bodies and their minds.

The New Birth is not a rebirth of the human *body*, but a rebirth of the human *spirit*. And the infilling of the Holy Spirit is not a physical experience, but a spiritual experience.

Paul said we have to present our bodies to God a living sacrifice.

We have to get our minds renewed with the Word.

Notice that this is something that we do—not God. God gives eternal life. He offers us His Spirit. But God doesn't do anything with our bodies. If anything is done with them, we have to do it.

The Word says that *you* present your body unto God. Nobody else can do it for you. The Word says that *you* are to be *"transformed by the renewing of your mind."* Our minds are renewed through the Word of God.

We know that man is a spirit, made in the image and likeness of God. Some people believe that man is just an animal. However, if that were true, it wouldn't be any more wrong to kill a man and eat him than it would be to kill a cow and eat it! Man has a physical body that he is living in, but he is not an animal. He is more than just mind and body. He is spirit, soul and body. He is a spirit; he has a soul; and he lives in a body. Animals have souls, but they are not spirits. There is nothing in animals that is like God.

God took something of Himself and put it in man. He made the body of man out of the dust of the earth, but He breathed into man's nostrils the breath of life.

The word "breath," or *ruach* in the Hebrew, means breath or spirit, and is translated "Holy Spirit" many times in the Old Testament. God is a spirit, so He took something of Himself—spirit—and put it into man. When He did, man became a living soul. He wasn't alive until then. He became a living soul. He became conscious of himself, because the body was dead without the spirit.

The soul possesses intellectual and emotional qualities, and animals have souls. But when their physical bodies are dead, they are dead.

Human souls—our intellectual and emotional qualities—are not based upon the physical, but upon the spirit; and when our body is dead, our soul still exists.

### LUKE 16:19–25

19 There was a certain rich man, which was clothed in purple and fine linen, and fared sumptuously every day:
20 And there was a certain beggar named Lazarus, which was laid at his gate, full of sores,
21 And desiring to be fed with the crumbs which fell from the rich man's table: moreover the dogs came and licked his sores.
22 And it came to pass, that the beggar died, and was carried by the angels into Abraham's bosom: the rich man also died, and was buried;
23 And in hell he lift up his eyes, being in torments, and seeth Abraham afar off, and Lazarus in his bosom.

24 And he cried and said, Father Abraham, have mercy on me, and send Lazarus, that he may dip the tip of his finger in water, and cool my tongue; for I am tormented in this flame.
25 But Abraham said, Son, remember that thou in thy lifetime receivedst thy good things, and likewise Lazarus evil things: but now he is comforted, and thou art tormented.

In this passage of Scripture we have a very vivid illustration of man's three parts: spirit, soul, and body. Notice verse 22 says, *"the beggar died and was carried by the angels into Abraham's bosom."* Who was carried away? (The beggar. Not his body, but *he*.) His spirit is the real person. His body was put in the grave, but *he* was in "Abraham's bosom."

The rich man also died. His body was put in the grave, but *"in hell he lift up his eyes."* Although Abraham's body had been in the grave many years, the rich man saw *him*. He also recognized Lazarus. Therefore, in the spirit realm, man looks very similar to what he does in this life.

The rich man cried out to Abraham, *". . . have mercy on me, and send Lazarus, that he may dip the tip of his finger in water, and cool my tongue; for I am tormented in this flame. But Abraham said, Son, remember. . . ."*

Man is a spirit, and he has a soul. We see in this scripture that his soul is still intact. He can still remember. He has emotion. He was tormented. He was concerned about his five brothers still living (vv. 27–28).

God is a spirit. He became a man, for Jesus was God manifested in the flesh, living in a human body. He took on a physical body, and when He did, He was no less God than He was before.

We know that man leaves his physical body at death, and when he does he is no less man than he was when he had his physical body, as proved by the story of the rich man and Lazarus.

We cannot know God through our human knowledge—through our mind. God is only revealed to man through his spirit. It is the spirit of man that contacts God, for God is a spirit.

---

**Memory Text:**
"For with the heart man believeth unto righteousness; and with the mouth confession is made unto salvation."
—Rom. 10:10

---

# What It Means to Believe With the Heart
## (Part 2)

**Bible Texts:** 2 Corinthians 5:1,6–8; Proverbs 3:5–7

**Central Truth:** To believe with all of our heart is to believe with our spirit, independently of our mind or our body.

Spiritual things are just as real as material things. God is just as real as if He had a physical body, although He doesn't. He is a spirit.

Jesus has a physical body now—a flesh-and-bone body—but not flesh and blood. After His resurrection, He appeared to the disciples, and they thought He was a spirit (or ghost). But Jesus said, *"handle me . . . for a spirit hath not flesh and bones . . ."* (Luke 24:39).

On another occasion, while Peter and some of the other disciples were fishing, they saw Jesus on the shore. He called them, and they went to Him and ate fish He was cooking on an open fire.

He has a physical body now—a resurrected flesh-and-bone body. And Jesus, who is now in heaven with His physical body, is not *more* real than the Holy Spirit or God the Father are real.

Notice we do not say God is spirit, but rather that God is a spirit. Some people think that God is spirit, meaning some sort of an impersonal influence. Even though we say that God is a spirit, that doesn't mean He doesn't have a shape or a form in the spiritual realm, because He does. Angels are spirits, yet angels have a form, or a spirit body.

On one occasion when the Israelites were surrounded by the Syrian army, the servant of the prophet Elisha was filled with fear as he saw the enemy's host of horses and chariots which compassed the city. Elisha merely answered, *"Fear not: for they that be with us are more than they that be with them. And Elisha prayed, and said, Lord . . . open his eyes, that he may see. And the Lord opened the eyes of the young man; and he saw: and, behold, the mountain was full of* horses and chariots of fire round about Elisha" (2 Kings 6:16–17). Sometimes, as God wills, angels can take on a form in the material realm where they can be seen.

In Exodus 33 we read that God talked to Moses "face to face" (v. 11), although Moses did not see God's face, because a cloud was there. "Thou canst not see my face: for there shall no man see me, and live" (v. 20).

Then God said to Moses, "And it shall come to pass, while my glory passeth by, that I will put thee in a clift of the rock, and will cover thee with my hand while I pass by: And I will take away mine hand, and thou shalt see my back parts: but my face shall not be seen" (vv. 22–23).

Even though God is a spirit, we know that He has a face and hands—a form of some kind. He is no less real because He is a spirit than He would be if He had a physical body. Spiritual things are just as real as material things.

**2 CORINTHIANS 5:1,6–8**
**1 For we know that if our earthly house of this tabernacle were dissolved, we have a building of God, an house not made with hands, eternal in the heavens. . . .**
**6 Therefore we are always confident, knowing that, whilst we are at home in the body, we are absent from the Lord:**
**7 (For we walk by faith, not by sight:)**

**8 We are confident, I say, and willing rather to be absent from the body, and to be present with the Lord.**

When our body is put in the grave, we still have a building with God that is not made with hands, and we shall live eternally in the heavens. Who is going to be absent from the body? We are— the real man—the inward man.

In First Peter 3:4 our spirit is called "the hidden man of the heart." Here we see the word "heart" again. The inward man—our spirit—is called the hidden man. He is a man of the heart, of the spirit. He is hidden to the physical or the natural man. In Romans 7:22 the spirit is called the "inward man." ("For I delight in the law of God after the inward man.") So we see this "inward man" and the "hidden man" give us God's definition of the human spirit.

The real man is spirit; he has a body and a soul. With his *spirit* he contacts the spiritual realm. With his *soul* he contacts the intellectual realm. With his *body* he contacts the physical realm.

We cannot contact God with our mind. Neither can we contact God with our body. We can contact God only with our spirit.

### The Word of God— Key to Heart Faith

When we hear the Word of God preached, we hear it with our natural mind. (Before we were Christians, the Holy Spirit, through the Word, spoke to our heart or our spirit.) We read in First Corinthians 2:14, *"The natural man receiveth not the things of the Spirit of God . . ."* One translation says, "The natural man or the natural mind understandeth not the things of the Spirit of God, for they are foolishness unto him. Neither can he know them because they are spiritually discerned."

We don't understand the Bible with our mind. It is spiritually understood. We understand it with our spirit, or our heart. That is the reason we may read certain passages dozens of times and never understand their true meaning. Then one day we suddenly see what God is showing us through His Word. It is at that moment that we understand it with our heart. We have to get the revelation of God's Word in our heart. That is why we must depend upon the Spirit of God to open and unveil the Word to us.

Therefore, to believe with the heart means to believe with the spirit. How does our spirit get faith that our intellect cannot obtain? The answer is: through the Word.

When Jesus said, *". . . Man shall not live by bread alone, but by every word that proceedeth out of the mouth of God"* (Matt. 4:4), He was speaking of spiritual food. He used a natural term to convey a spiritual thought.

Our spirit becomes filled with assurance and confidence as we meditate on the Word. The Word is spirit and faith food. The Word of God is food that makes our spirit strong.

To believe with the heart means to believe apart from what our physical body may tell us, or what our physical senses may indicate. This is because the physical man believes what he sees with his physical eyes, hears with his physical ears, or feels through his physical senses. But the spirit, or heart, believes in the Word regardless of seeing, hearing, or feeling.

**PROVERBS 3:5–7**
**5  Trust in the Lord with all thine heart; and lean not unto thine own understanding.**
**6  In all thy ways acknowledge him, and he shall direct thy paths.**
**7  Be not wise in thine own eyes: fear the Lord, and depart from evil.**

Most people practice verse 5 all right, but they practice it in reverse. They trust with all their understanding and lean not to their own heart! James 1:19 says, *". . . let every man be swift to hear, slow to speak, slow to wrath."* This is another verse we are inclined to practice in reverse. We are swift to speak and swift to wrath, but slow to hear.

Then verse 7 in the above passage of Scripture says, *"Be not wise in thine own eyes . . ."* In other words, "Don't be wise with natural human knowledge,

31

which would cause you to act independently of the Word of God."

In the New Testament we find the counterpart of this scripture. *"(For the weapons of our warfare are not carnal, but mighty through God to the pulling down of strong holds;) Casting down imaginations* [reasoning], *and every high thing that exalteth itself against the knowledge of God, and bringing into captivity every thought to the obedience of Christ"* (2 Cor. 10:4–5).

## Peace—A Result of Heart Faith

If we want to walk by faith, the Word must be uppermost to everything else. And as we trust God with all our heart, a quietness and a peace come to our spirit. *"For we which have believed do enter into rest . . ."* (Heb. 4:3). *"And the peace of God, which passeth all understanding, shall keep your hearts and minds through Christ Jesus"* (Phil. 4:7). *"Thou wilt keep him in perfect peace, whose mind is stayed on thee: because he trusteth in thee"* (Isa. 26:3).

God's Word says, *"But my God shall supply all your need according to his riches in glory by Christ Jesus"* (Phil. 4:19). We know in our spirit that everything we need will be supplied. We don't worry. We have no anxiety. If we are worrying, we are not believing. Our heart takes courage as we read the Word. As we meditate in this Word, our assurance becomes deeper. This assurance in our spirit is independent of human reasoning or human knowledge. It may even contradict human reasoning or physical evidence. *But to believe God with our heart means to believe apart from our body.*

Dr. Lilian Yeomans said, "God delights in His children stepping out over the aching void with nothing underneath their feet but the Word of God."

The reason why many people are defeated is because they accept defeat. But God's Word says, *"Ye are of God, little children, and have overcome them: because greater is he that is in you, than he that is in the world"* (1 John 4:4). The Holy Spirit rises up in us, and we know we cannot be conquered. We know because we *believe!*

---

**Memory Text:**
"Trust in the Lord with all thine heart; and lean not unto thine own understanding."
—Prov. 3:5

---

# Faith for Prosperity

**Bible Texts:** Galatians 3:13-14,29; Deuteronomy 28:1-8,11-12

**Central Truth:** As born-again believers, we are redeemed from the curse of the law and are heirs to Abraham's blessing and God's promises of prosperity.

For many years I did not understand that it is God's will for His children to prosper. I thought, as many do, that poverty is a characteristic of humility—and in order to be humble, one must be poor.

I thought that a righteous man could not be wealthy, and a wealthy man could not be righteous.

I thought any promise in the Scriptures regarding financial blessing applied only to the Jews. I have since learned, through studying God's Word and applying it in my own life, that God wants His children to *"prosper and be in health, even as thy soul prospereth"* (3 John 2).

Someone might say, "The Bible says that money is the root of all evil." However, the Bible does not say that at all. First Timothy 6:10 says, *"For THE LOVE OF MONEY is the root of all evil: which*

*while some coveted after, they have erred from the faith, and pierced themselves through with many sorrows."* A person can be guilty of that sin and not have one dime!

I have heard people say, "Well, I guess I'm just another Job." Some people think that poor old Job went through life poverty-stricken, sick, and afflicted. However, the entire Book of Job happened within a period of nine months, and the last chapter says God turned Job's captivity, and *"the Lord gave Job twice as much as he had before"* (Job 42:10).

When the thieves broke in and stole Job's things, he was in captivity to Satan. When the fire fell and burned up his crops, he was in captivity to Satan. When the storm came and blew the house down on his children and they were killed; when Job was smitten with boils from his head to his feet; when his wife turned against him and said, "Curse God and die," Job was in captivity to Satan. But God turned Job's captivity.

If you think you are another Job, that means you'll be one of the richest men around! You'll have twice as much as you've ever had before. You will be healed and live to be old. (Job lived 140 years after the events recorded in the Bible.) If you are another Job, you will prosper.

## Redeemed From the Curse of the Law

GALATIANS 3:13–14,29
**13 Christ hath redeemed us from the curse of the law, being made a curse for us: for it is written, Cursed is every one that hangeth on a tree: 14 That the blessing of Abraham might come on the Gentiles through Jesus Christ; that we might receive the promise of the Spirit through faith. . . . 29 And if ye be Christ's, then are ye Abraham's seed, and heirs according to the promise.**

The above scriptures tell us that Christ has redeemed us from the curse of the law. What, then, is the curse of the law? We turn for this answer to the first five books of the Old Testament, referred to as the Pentateuch, or the books of the Law. There we learn that the curse, or punishment, for breaking

God's law is threefold: poverty, sickness, and the second death.

Christ has redeemed us from the curse of poverty. He has redeemed us from the curse of sickness. He has redeemed us from the curse of death—spiritual death now and physical death when Jesus comes again. We need have no fear of the second death.

## Abraham's Blessing

Just as the curse is threefold in nature, so was Abraham's blessing. First, it was a material, financial blessing. Second, it was a physical blessing. Third, it was a spiritual blessing.

The New Testament scripture Third John 2 agrees that God wants us to have material, physical, and spiritual prosperity, because it says, *"Beloved, I wish above all things that thou mayest prosper and be in health, even as thy soul prospereth."* Too many people are under the impression that any promises in the Bible for material blessing and prosperity refer only to the Jews. However, this verse was written to New Testament Christians.

The word "Jew" is a short term or nickname for "Judah." The Israelites were never called Jews until after the split of the tribes. Judah didn't have any more promise of material and financial blessing than the other tribes of Israel. They received or inherited the blessing through their father Jacob. Jacob inherited the blessing through his father Isaac. Isaac inherited the blessing through his father Abraham. So it is not the Jews' blessing or promise. It is not Israel's blessing. *It is Abraham's blessing.* And that blessing is mine! *"That the blessing of Abraham might come on the Gentiles through Jesus Christ . . ."* (Gal. 3:14). In this third chapter of Galatians we also read, *"Know ye therefore that they which are of faith, the same are the children of Abraham"* (v. 7). If we are born-again Christians, *"then are ye Abraham's seed, and heirs according to the promise"* (Gal. 3:29).

After these scriptures became plain to me and I saw what belonged to me as a child of God through faith in Him, other scriptures began to open up to me. Everything belongs to God and is at His disposal.

*"For every beast of the forest is mine, and the cattle upon a thousand hills . . . for the world is mine, and the fulness thereof"* (Ps. 50:10,12). *"The earth is the Lord's, and the fulness thereof . . ."* (Ps. 24: 1).

God created everything; then He made man, Adam, and gave him dominion over all of it. God made it all for His man Adam. He gave Adam dominion over the cattle on a thousand hills, over the silver and gold, over the world and the fullness thereof. In other words, Adam was the god of this world.

But Adam committed high treason and sold out to Satan. Thus, Satan became the god of this world. Jesus, however, came to redeem us from Satan's power and dominion over us. Romans 5:17 says, *"For if by one man's offence death reigned by one; much more they which receive abundance of grace and of the gift of righteousness shall reign in life by one, Jesus Christ."*

*The Amplified* version of this scripture reads, *"For if, because of one man's trespass (lapse, offense) death reigned through that one, much more surely will those who receive [God's] overflowing grace (unmerited favor) and the free gift of righteousness [putting them into right standing with Himself] reign as kings in life through the one Man Jesus Christ (the Messiah, the Anointed One)."*

We are to reign as kings in life. That means that we have dominion over our lives. We are to dominate, not be dominated. Circumstances are not to dominate us. We are to dominate circumstances. Poverty is not to rule and reign over us. We are to rule and reign over poverty. Disease and sickness are not to rule and reign over us. We are to rule and reign over sickness. We are to reign as kings in life by Christ Jesus, in whom we have redemption.

**DEUTERONOMY 28:1–8,11–12**
**1   And it shall come to pass, if thou shalt hearken diligently unto the voice**

of the Lord thy God, to observe and to do all his commandments which I command thee this day, that the Lord thy God will set thee on high above all nations of the earth:

2 And all these blessings shall come on thee, and overtake thee, if thou shalt hearken unto the voice of the Lord thy God.

3 Blessed shalt thou be in the city, and blessed shalt thou be in the field.

4 Blessed shall be the fruit of thy body, and the fruit of thy ground, and the fruit of thy cattle . . .

5 Blessed shall be thy basket and thy store.

6 Blessed shalt thou be when thou comest in, and blessed shalt thou be when thou goest out.

7 The Lord shall cause thine enemies that rise up against thee to be smitten before thy face . . .

8 The Lord shall command the blessing upon thee in thy storehouses, and in all that thou settest thine hand unto . . .

11 And the Lord shall make thee plenteous in goods . . .

12 The Lord shall open unto thee his good treasure, the heaven to give the rain unto thy land in his season, and to bless all the work of thine hand . . .

The first part of Deuteronomy 28 lists the many ways the Lord would bless His people if they would obey Him. He promised to bless their children, their crops, and cattle. He promised to bless and protect them in battle.

He promised to make them "plenteous in goods," and to bless them in "all that thou settest thine hand unto."

This blessing was all-inclusive, but it also was conditional. They must keep all of God's commandments. They must be a holy people, not straying from Him and seeking after other gods, but serving Him with all their hearts. The remainder of this chapter, verses 15 through 68, lists the curses that would fall upon His people if they did not keep His commandments.

When I first realized this truth and saw the prosperity, material and spiritual, that God has planned for His people, and that every born-again believer in Christ is an heir to this promise, I could hardly contain my joy!

I was thrilled to find out that I was redeemed from the curse of the law, from the curse of poverty, and that Abraham's blessing was mine.

We as Christians need not suffer financial setbacks; we need not be captive to poverty or sickness! God has provided healing and prosperity for His children if they will obey His commandments.

When Jesus was here on earth He said, *"If ye then, being evil, know how to give good gifts unto your children, HOW MUCH MORE shall your Father which is in heaven give good things to them that ask him?"* (Matt. 7:11).

How many of us who are parents want our children to go through life hungry, sick, or afflicted, never having enough to get along? No parent wants that. In fact, we work and sacrifice to try to help our children get a better education than we had so they can make a better living than we did.

God put all the cattle here; all the silver and gold. Is it reasonable to think that He did all of this only for the ungodly? Certainly He loves the sinner, but does He love the sinner more than His own children? No. God put all these things here for His people.

He said to Israel, *"If ye be willing and obedient, ye shall eat the good of the land"* (Isa. 1:19). And if God wants His children to eat the best, He wants them to wear the best clothing; He wants them to drive the best cars; He wants them to have the best of everything.

## Proved Through Personal Experience

When this truth became real to my heart, the Lord spoke to me and said, "Don't pray for money anymore. You have authority through my Name to claim prosperity. I already have put gold, silver, and cattle on a thousand hills for my man Adam, and I gave him dominion over it. After he sold out to Satan, the second Adam, Jesus Christ, came to redeem you from the hand of the enemy and to remove you from the curse of the law. Now, instead of praying that I would do it, because I have made provision for your needs, all you need to do is say, 'Satan, take your hands off my money.' Just claim what you need. You reign in life by Christ Jesus."

At this time in my life, I was an evangelist. At the next church I went to I said, "Lord, to get what I need here, this will have to work. The last time I was here I received only about $60 a week. I am going to claim $150 for this week." Then I said, "Satan, take your hands off my money in the Name of the Lord Jesus Christ."

You see, you never believe for the possible; you believe for the impossible. I was supposed to be in this church for just a week, but as it turned out, I was there ten days. I claimed $200 for these ten days. The pastor did not beg for money at all; he simply passed the offering plates, and when the offering was counted I had $240.

After that when I would go into churches to hold meetings, finances came in easily, and many times the pastor would say in amazement, "That is the biggest offering this church has ever given to an evangelist." And I had made no strong pleas at all. I had the key that unlocks the door.

Thank God, we are not under the curse, because Jesus has set us free!

"For sickness I have health, for poverty wealth, since Jesus has ransomed me."

---

### Memory Text:
"Beloved, I wish above all things that thou mayest prosper and be in health, even as thy soul prospereth."

—3 John 2

---

# Seven Steps to the Highest Kind of Faith
## (Part 1)

**Bible Texts:** Colossians 1:12–14; 1 Corinthians 6:19–20

**Central Truth:** It is by the blood of the Lamb and the word of our testimony that we overcome Satan, we are delivered from the power of darkness, and we are translated into the kingdom of His dear Son.

I have a twofold purpose in mind in this series of lessons on faith. We already have covered most of these next points in some form or another, but I wanted to bring them together so you can check up on the progress you are making.

If you have studied these faith lessons and they have taken hold in your life, the devil is going to contest you. The Lord wants you to be prepared for the future, and through the power of God's Word you can be ready for any emergency that may arise.

### Step One—The Integrity of the Word of God

The first thing you need to know is that the Word of God is actually what it declares itself to be. It is a revelation from God to us. It is God speaking to us *now*. Not only is it a book of the past and a book of the future; it also is a book of *now*. This book is a God-breathed, God-indwelt, and God-inspired message.

*"For the word of God is quick, and powerful, and sharper than any two-edged sword, piercing even to the dividing asunder of soul and spirit, and of the joints and marrow, and is a discerner of the thoughts and intents of the heart"* (Heb. 4:12). Moffatt's translation of this verse reads, *"For the Logos [Word] of God is a living thing . . ."* The word "quick" actually means "alive, living." The Word of God is a living thing. But it will only come alive to you as you accept it and act upon it.

So we see that the first step toward the highest kind of faith is to accept and understand the integrity of God's Word. The Word is of foremost importance.

Some people think God hasn't spoken to them unless they have a message in tongues or prophecy. But the Word of God *is* God speaking to us.

The gifts of prophecy, tongues, and interpretation of tongues do not supersede the Word. The Word comes first. These inspirational vocal gifts are given to us to inspire us in line with the Word, but if they say something apart from the Word, it is not the Holy Spirit speaking; that person is just speaking from his own thinking. You always must judge these things in the light of God's Word.

Also, there are those who try to read certain things into the Word because they want it to say what they believe. They are trying to fit the Word to their beliefs rather than fitting their beliefs to the Word.

Some people try to overlook certain passages or explain them away. But you must accept the Word for what it says and walk in the light of it. You must believe what the Word says, not what you *think* it says.

As you begin to study the Word in this light, accepting it as it is, you will be amazed to learn that some of the things you always have believed are not in the Word at all. You will wonder why you believed some things the way you did.

I found this true in my own experience. As I lay for many months on the bed of sickness, studying the Bible, I saw in it truths of faith and healing. These were new to me, because my church didn't teach about healing. But the more I studied God's Word, the more I saw it was true. And regardless of my church's teaching, I determined I was going to walk in the light of God's Word, because I believed that this Word is God speaking to us today. When I made this commitment, the biggest part of the battle was won.

To actually believe God's Word, I had to go against not only the teachings of my church but of my family as well. It is amazing how we can become more church-minded than Bible-minded. And sometimes our loved ones, thinking they have our best interests at heart, will oppose us from walking in the fullest light of God's Word. Nevertheless, I determined to follow the Word of God, knowing that this is God speaking to me today.

## Step Two—Our Redemption in Christ

The second thing you need to know is the reality of our redemption in Christ—not as a doctrine, philosophy, or creed of some kind—but an actual redemption from the authority of Satan. By the New Birth we have been translated into the kingdom of His Son, the Kingdom of God. In other words, we have been born into the very family of God.

**COLOSSIANS 1:12–14**

**12 Giving thanks unto the Father, which hath made us meet [able] to be partakers of the inheritance of the saints in light:**

**13 Who hath delivered us from the power of darkness, and hath translated us into the kingdom of his dear Son:**

**14 In whom we have redemption through his blood, even the forgiveness of sins.**

How wonderful that we *can* enter into our inheritance in Christ. God has made us *able* to have part of this inheritance, as we have just read.

Verse 13 goes on to say, *"Who hath delivered us from the power of darkness . . ."* The Greek word translated "power" here means "authority." *"Who hath delivered us from the AUTHORITY of darkness . . ."* refers to Satan's kingdom. Notice, too, that the scripture doesn't say that He is going to deliver us. It says, *"Who HATH delivered us . . ."*

Verse 14 tells us the price of redemption. *"In whom we have redemption through his blood . . ."* In connection with this scripture let us look at Revelation 12:11, *"And they overcame him by the blood of the Lamb, and by the word of their testimony . . ."* The *American Standard Version* of this verse reads, *". . . because of the blood of the Lamb, and because of the word of their testimony."*

The blood of Jesus is the basis for our victory. But we have to add our testimony, our confession, to it. We have to stand our ground with the enemy.

Because Satan is the god of this world, he will try to have authority over you. But he needn't win, because you have been delivered through the blood of Jesus Christ from the power of darkness; from the authority of Satan. By virtue of the New Birth, you have been translated into the kingdom of His dear Son. In every contest with Satan you can overcome, no matter what the test may be, because you have redemption through the blood of the Lamb and because of the word of your testimony.

### There Is Power in the Blood!

Satan's dominion over us as new creatures in Christ is ended. Jesus is the Lord and Head of this new Body. He is referred to in the Scriptures as the Head of the Church. The Church, which is all born-again believers, is called the Body of Christ. Satan has no right to rule over the Body of Christ. Christ is the Head of the Body. He is the One who is to rule and dominate the Body.

Some people accept defeat in life because they don't fully understand the Word. They have told me that they didn't succeed because it wasn't God's will. They have said, "Our spirits belong to the Lord, but our bodies haven't been redeemed as yet. Therefore, we must suffer sickness and disease in the physical realm now. But the time is coming when we won't have to." In answer to this I turn to First Corinthians 6.

**1 CORINTHIANS 6:19–20**
**19 What? know ye not that your body is the temple of the Holy Ghost which is in you, which ye have of God, and ye are not your own?**
**20 For ye are bought with a price: therefore glorify God in your body, and in your spirit, which are God's.**

This passage tells us that not only our spirit, but also our body is bought with a price. Therefore you are to *"glorify God in your body and in your spirit which are God's."* Does God get any glory out of Satan's dominating us physically? Could God get any glory out of the body, the temple of the Holy Spirit, which is deformed or defaced with sickness? Certainly not. We need to understand this clearly, and we need to learn to take a stand against the devil when he attacks our bodies—just as we would when he attacks our spirits.

Let us look again at Colossians 1:12, *"Giving thanks unto the Father, which hath made us meet* [able] *to be partakers of the inheritance of the saints in light."* This is part of our inheritance as children of God as we walk in the light. We have dominion and authority over the devil through the blood of Jesus. It is by the blood of the Lamb *and* the word of our testimony that we overcome Satan, we are delivered from the power of darkness, and we are translated into the kingdom of His dear Son.

Notice the words, *"Giving thanks unto the Father, which hath made us ABLE to be partakers of the inheritance . . ."* We can partake of our inheritance right now. We don't have to relegate that to the future. We have an inheritance now. We have deliverance and redemption from the hand of Satan *now.* We can overcome him *now* by the blood of the Lamb and by the word of our testimony. We can glorify God *now* in our bodies and in our spirits, which are God's.

---

### Memory Text:
"And they overcame him
by the blood of the Lamb, and
by the word
of their testimony. . . ."
—Rev. 12:11

---

# Seven Steps to the Highest Kind of Faith
## (Part 2)

**Bible Texts:** 2 Corinthians 5:17;
1 John 1:3-4,7; John 14:13-14

**Central Truth:** Fellowship is the very mother of faith.
It is the parent of joy. It is the source of victory.

As we press on in our study of God's Word toward a deeper understanding of the meaning of faith, let us examine three more steps to the highest kind of faith.

These steps will impress on us the reality of: (1) the new creation, (2) our fellowship with the Father, and (3) the authority of Jesus' Name.

### Step Three—The Reality of the New Creation

**2 CORINTHIANS 5:17**
**17 Therefore if any man be in Christ, he is a new creature: old things are passed away; behold, all things are become new.**

To achieve the highest kind of faith, it is necessary for us to know the reality of the new creation. We need to know that in the mind of God, we were created in Christ Jesus after He had been made sin as our Substitute.

We should know that the moment we accepted Christ as Savior and confessed Him as Lord, we were *recreated*. That is when the legal aspect became a reality in our life.

Today we have in our spirits the very life and nature of God. This is not an experience, it is not a religion, nor is it joining a church. It is an actual birth of our spirit.

We are the very sons and daughters of God. He is our very own Father. We know we have passed from Satan's dominion and spiritual death into the realm of life through Jesus Christ.

*"We know that we have passed from death unto life, because we love the brethren . . ."* (1 John 3:14). We know we are in the family of God. We

43

are children of God. One cannot join this family; he must be born into it.

How does this affect us in everyday life? If God is our very own Father and we are His very own children, we have as much freedom and fellowship with the Father as Jesus had in His earthly walk, because the Father loves us even as He loved Jesus! John 17:23 says, *". . . that the world may know that thou hast sent me, and hast loved them, AS THOU HAST LOVED ME."*

Colossians 1:18 says, *"And he is the head of the body, the church: who is the beginning, the firstborn from the dead; that in all things he might have the preeminence."* Jesus is the firstborn, but we, too, are born again from the dead.

Peter said, *"Being born again, not of corruptible seed, but of incorruptible, by the word of God, which liveth and abideth for ever"* (1 Peter 1:23)

We are begotten of God. We are born of God. We are God's children, heirs of God and joint (equal) heirs with Christ.

When we say this, we are not magnifying ourselves; we are magnifying God and what He has done for us through the Lord Jesus. We did not make ourselves new creatures; He made us new creatures. He is the Author and Finisher of our faith: *"For we are his workmanship, created in Christ Jesus unto good works . . ."* (Eph. 2:10).

We didn't make ourselves who and what we are; God did.

When a person belittles himself, he is actually belittling God's workmanship. He is criticizing something God has made. We should quit looking at ourselves from the natural standpoint, and instead see ourselves as God sees us, as created in Christ Jesus. The Father doesn't see us as anybody else sees us. He sees us in Christ.

Many Christians are defeated because they look at themselves from the natural standpoint. They could be victorious by looking at themselves as God does.

A Christian who was having severe problems in his life once said to me, "I guess I'm just paying for the life I lived before I got saved. I was so sinful." However, when we are born again, we are redeemed not only from sin, but from the penalty of sin. We do not have to pay for our sins; Christ already has done this for us. It is not even possible for us to pay for them.

Many people don't know the difference between repentance and doing penance. Yet if you would accuse them of following the teachings of certain other religions, they would hotly deny it. But that is exactly what they are doing—trying to do penance for their past life.

After a man repents, God no longer has any knowledge that that man ever did anything wrong! *"I, even I, am he* that blotteth out thy transgressions for mine own sake, and *WILL NOT REMEMBER THY SINS*" (Isa. 43:25). If God doesn't remember, why should you?

If after being saved, a man had to continue to reap what he had sown as a sinner, he would then have to go to hell when he died, because that's part of the penalty, too. If he is going to reap any part of the penalty, he will reap all of it. But we are redeemed not only from the power, but also from the penalty of sin. Jesus took our place. He suffered the penalty for our sin. He has made us able to enjoy the inheritance of saints in light, as we discussed in our last lesson.

## Step Four—The Reality of Our Fellowship With the Father

The very heart reason for redemption is fellowship. *"God is faithful, by whom ye were called unto the fellowship of his Son Jesus Christ our Lord"* (1 Cor. 1:9). Notice here that we were called ". . . *unto the fellowship of his Son."*

**1 JOHN 1:3–4,7**
**3 That which we have seen and heard declare we unto you, that ye also may have fellowship with us: and truly our fellowship is with the Father, and with his Son Jesus Christ.**
**4 And these things write we unto you, that your joy may be full . . .**
**7 But if we walk in the light, as he is in the light, we have fellowship one with another, and the blood of Jesus Christ his Son cleanseth us from all sin.**

The highest honor the Father has conferred upon us is that of having joint fellowship with Him, with His Son, and with the Holy Spirit in carrying out His dream for the redemption of the human race.

Relationship without fellowship is an insipid thing. It is like marriage without love or companionship.

Fellowship is the very mother of faith. It is the parent of joy. It is the source of victory. And He has called us individually into fellowship with His Son.

If we have fellowship with Him and we are walking in the light as He is in the light, then prayer becomes one of the sweetest and greatest privileges we have.

To hear some people talk, one would think prayer is pure drudgery. We hear them talk about fighting and struggling; about trying to believe. But it never has been a problem or a fight for me to pray. It always has been a joy. It never has taken anything out of me to pray; it puts something in me. I often pray five or more hours a day.

The trouble with people who have such difficulty with prayer is that instead of letting the Holy Spirit help them and pray through them, they try to do it all on their own—in their own energy. Naturally this wears them out. God wants us to come to the place of resting in Him: *"For with stammering lips and another tongue will he speak to this people. To whom he said, This is the rest wherewith ye may cause the weary to rest; and this is the refreshing . . ."* (Isa. 28:11–12). We can find a time of refreshing in the Lord as we pray in other tongues.

## Step Five—The Reality of the Authority of Jesus' Name

**JOHN 14:13–14**
**13 And whatsoever ye shall ask in my name, that will I do, that the Father may be glorified in the Son.**
**14 If ye shall ask any thing in my name, I will do it.**

Suppose a wealthy man were to give you a signed statement stating that you were entitled to use his name and thereby receive anything you might need in order to live comfortably.

Suppose this was a legal document, given before witnesses, whereby every one of your needs could be met for the rest of your life. Does this sound too good to be true? The wonderful part of it is that it *is* true!

God has given us "the power of attorney" to use the Name of Jesus to meet our every need: spiritual, physical, or financial. He has given us power over satanic forces. He has said He would give us "whatsoever ye shall ask in my name."

We have that authority to use His Name. The fact that many do not is not a matter of lack of faith, but a matter of not knowing our legal rights in Christ. It is a matter of taking the place of a son or daughter and taking advantage of our rights as a child of God. It is a matter of knowing what belongs to us and doing what the Word says.

---

**Memory Text:**
"God is faithful, by whom ye were called unto the fellowship of his Son
Jesus Christ our Lord."
—1 Cor. 1:9

---

# Seven Steps to the Highest Kind of Faith
## (Part 3)

**Bible Texts:** 2 Corinthians 6:14–16;
Romans 3:23–26; Psalm 32:1–2

**Central Truth:** We can approach God with full
assurance, because we have been made the
righteousness of God in Christ Jesus.

This lesson brings us to Step Six in our study of the highest faith. In it we want to help you gain new insight into the meaning of the words "righteous" and "righteousness," as shown in the Scriptures.

### Step Six—The Reality of Our Righteousness

**2 CORINTHIANS 6:14–16**
**14 Be ye not unequally yoked together with unbelievers: for what fellowship hath righteousness with unrighteousness? and what communion hath light with darkness?**
**15 And what concord hath Christ with Belial? or what part hath he that believeth with an infidel?**
**16 And what agreement hath the temple of God with idols? for ye are the temple of the living God; as God hath said, I will dwell in them, and walk in them; and I will be their God, and they shall be my people.**

Many people see in the above passage only a teaching about separation from the world, and they immediately practice *segregation*, thinking it is *separation*. They feel they cannot have anything to do with the world or anyone in the world. They even segregate themselves from other Christians if they don't completely agree with them.

However, Jesus said, *"Ye are the salt of the earth . . . Ye are the light of the world . . ."* (Matt. 5:13–14). In order to be the salt and light in the world, we must remain in the world, doing our job for the Lord.

A man once said to me, "I am the only Christian where I work. Pray that God will move me out."

"Oh, no," I told him. "The place would really be corrupt without your influence. You stay right there. You're the salt of the earth; you stay right there and salt it." We are *in* the world, but we are not *of* the world.

Notice something equally important about this passage: Believers are called "believers," and unbelievers are called "unbelievers." Believers are called "righteousness," and unbelievers are referred to as "unrighteousness." Believers are called "light" and unbelievers "darkness."

The idea of calling yourself "righteousness" sounds egotistical, yet people do not object to calling themselves "believers," or "light." This passage uses all three terms to refer to believers!

In verse 15 we see the Church, or believers, referred to as Christ, because He is the Head and we are the Body. And, of course, our head doesn't go by one name and our body by another. The Church is Christ, and we are the Body of Christ.

**ROMANS 3:23–26**
**23 For all have sinned, and come short of the glory of God;**
**24 Being justified freely by his grace through the redemption that is in Christ Jesus:**
**25 Whom God hath set forth to be a propitiation through faith in his blood, to declare his righteousness for the remission of sins that are past, through the forbearance of God;**
**26 To declare, I say, at this time his righteousness: that he might be just, and the justifier of him which believeth in Jesus.**

In this passage, the Greek word that can be translated "righteousness" or "righteous" is translated "just" and "justifier." In other words, verse 26 could just as easily read, "that he might be *righteous*, and the *righteousness* of him which believeth in Jesus."

What does all this mean? What is God teaching us through this scripture? That God through Jesus declared His righteousness. That God Himself is righteous, and that God is my righteousness. He is the "righteousness of him which believeth in Jesus."

Romans 5:17 says, *"For if by one man's offence death reigned by one; much more they which receive abundance of grace and of the gift of righteousness shall reign in life by one, Jesus Christ."*

Most people have thought that righteousness is something a person attains by right living. Righteousness does mean rightness or right standing, but this scripture says it is a *gift*—not something we can earn by good deeds and clean living.

A *gift* is something we receive instantly; a stage of spiritual development is *fruit*. If righteousness were fruit, the scripture would read, "and the fruit of righteousness." However, it says, "the *gift* of righteousness."

Every one of God's dear children has the same righteousness and standing with God. He doesn't love one person more than another. He doesn't listen to one person's prayers more than another's. When this truth fully sinks in, your prayers will work! Your prayers will get answered!

Many people struggle along in the realm of self-condemnation, allowing the enemy to rob them of the inheritance that is theirs in Christ Jesus. They think their prayers won't work and God won't hear them. They think if they could just find a righteous man to pray for them, his prayers would work.

How sad they have not seen the truths in the scriptures we just read. God is our righteousness. He became our righteousness when He imparted His nature, eternal life, to us when we were born again. He became our righteousness the moment we accepted Jesus as our Savior and confessed Him as our Lord.

I first discovered the truths of these scriptures as I lay bedfast for 16 months as a teenager. I did not understand these scriptures then. At first they were a small gleam of light in a dark corner. I was having the same struggles many of you have to overcome problems in your life or health.

Reading my Bible, one day I came across James 5:14–15: *"Is any sick among you? let him call for the elders of the church; and let them pray over him, anointing him with oil in the name of the Lord: And the prayer of faith shall save the sick, and the Lord shall raise him up; and if he have*

*committed any sins, they shall be forgiven him."*

As I read, any faith that momentarily flickered in my heart was quickly extinguished by the thought that my church didn't believe in healing or anointing with oil.

Then the Lord spoke to me and said, "It is *the prayer of faith* that heals the sick. You can pray that prayer yourself as well as anybody can."

I was just a babe in Christ. I was 16 years old and had been saved only a few months, yet the Lord said I could pray that prayer! But immediately my wrong thinking defeated me. I thought, *Yes, I could—if I were righteous.* (I was acquainted with all my shortcomings, and I knew I wasn't righteous; at least not according to my understanding of the word.)

Reading further in James, I read where Elijah is an example of a righteous man praying: *"Elias was a man subject to like passions as we are, and he prayed earnestly that it might not rain: and it rained not on the earth by the space of three years and six months"* (James 5:17).

As I studied about Elijah, I decided he was not my idea of a righteous man. When the hand of the Lord was upon him, he could outrun the king's chariot. But when he learned that Queen Jezebel wanted to kill him, he ran and hid under a juniper tree, begging the Lord to let him die. Then he whined to the Lord, "Everybody has backslidden but me. I'm the only one who is serving You, Lord."

Such inconsistency is hardly the mark of a righteous man. I wondered, *How could James have given him as an example of a righteous man praying? He was no more righteous than I!*

Then I remembered James said Elijah was *"a man subject to like passions as we are."* Not only was he subject to these passions; he also gave in to them. Even though he allowed discouragement to dominate his actions, he was called a righteous man.

## A Better Covenant

**PSALM 32:1–2**
**1 Blessed is he whose transgression is forgiven, whose sin is covered.**
**2 Blessed is the man unto whom the Lord imputeth not iniquity, and in whose spirit there is no guile.**

Under the Old Covenant, the blood of innocent animals covered sin. God did not impute iniquity to people, even though they had sinned. He covered their sin, forgave it, and imputed righteousness to them. In His sight, they were righteous. *". . . When I see the blood, I will pass over you,"* He said in Exodus 12:13.

If God did this for His children under the law, how much more will He do for us? Under grace we have a better covenant, established upon better promises. The blood of Jesus Christ not only covers our sins; it cleanses us "from all unrighteousness." Revelation 1:5 says, *". . . Unto him that loved us, and washed us from our sins in his own blood."*

As I read this scripture, I saw that when I had been born again, all my sins were remitted, and my past life ceased. I saw that I had become a new creature in Christ, and I knew He didn't make any unrighteous new creatures.

Immediately the devil was right there, saying, "That may be true, but what about since then? It wasn't very long ago that you lost your temper. That's certainly no way for a righteous person to act." He got me looking at the natural again instead of at God's Word.

Then I read First John 1:9, *"If we confess our sins, he is faithful and just to forgive us our sins, and to cleanse us from all unrighteousness."* (This scripture wasn't written to sinners, but to believers.)

This meant I became the righteousness of God in Christ when I was born again. If I had sinned since that time— and I had—I just confessed my sins and He forgave me and cleansed me from my unrighteousness. (If I'm cleansed from unrighteousness, then I'm righteous again.)

Before this, when I had read James 5:16—*". . . The effectual fervent prayer of a righteous man availeth much"*—I had thought if I could ever become righteous, I would have a tremendous prayer life and see out-standing answers to prayer.

Now I saw that my prayers would work, because God would hear me as quickly as He would anybody else. In my Bible, beside James 5:16, I wrote the words, "I am that Righteous Man."

This is not bragging on anything I have done; it is bragging on what I am in Christ. It is praising God for what He has wrought for us in Christ.

*This means we can stand in God's presence without any sense of guilt, condemnation, or inferiority.* This means the prayer problem is settled. No longer do we need to go into God's presence tongue-tied because of con-demnation, or filled with fear because of ignorance.

We can enter His presence in full assurance because we have been made righteous through the blood of our Lord Jesus Christ.

---

### Memory Text:

"For he hath made him to be sin for us, who knew no sin; that we might be made the righteousness of God in him."
—2 Cor. 5:21

---

# Seven Steps to the Highest Kind of Faith
## (Part 4)

**Bible Texts:** 1 Corinthians 6:19-20;
2 Corinthians 6:16; Acts 8:14-15; 9:17; 19:1-2

**Central Truth:** God Himself, in the person of the
Holy Spirit, dwells within the believer.

Too often those who have been filled with the Holy Spirit think they have received simply a wonderful blessing, or some kind of rich spiritual experience. They miss the teaching of the Word entirely. First John 4:4 says, *". . . greater is he that is in you, than he that is in the world."*

The infilling of the Holy Spirit means that He—the Holy Spirit—comes to dwell in us. Jesus said, *"And I will pray the Father, and he shall give you another Comforter, that HE MAY ABIDE WITH YOU FOR EVER"* (John 14:16).

Therefore, the seventh—and an extremely vital—step in our search for the highest kind of faith is to realize that our body is the temple of God. *God Himself, in the person of the Holy Spirit, dwells within us!*

## Step Seven—The Reality of the Indwelling Spirit

In Old Testament times, God's earthly dwelling place was the tabernacle, or Temple. But since Christ died on the cross, rose again, and returned to heaven, sending the Holy Spirit upon the believers on the Day of Pentecost, He no longer dwells in a man-made Holy of Holies. Our bodies have become His temple!

**1 CORINTHIANS 6:19–20**

**19 What? know ye not that your body is the temple of the Holy Ghost which is in you, which ye have of God, and ye are not your own?**

**20 For ye are bought with a price: therefore glorify God in your body, and in your spirit, which are God's.**

**2 CORINTHIANS 6:16**
16 . . . for ye are the temple of the living God; as God hath said, I will dwell in them, and walk in them; and I will be their God, and they shall be my people.

In every crisis of life, we should instinctively say, "I am a conqueror. I am more than a victor, for the Creator dwells in me. The Greater One lives in me. He can put me over. He can make me a success. I cannot fail!" This is not bragging on yourself. It is bragging on the One who is in you.

Too often, however, Spirit-filled believers cringe before the trials of life, and needlessly allow the devil to defeat them. They run around crying on one another's shoulders, praying pitiful, weak little prayers, wondering why victory doesn't come. Yet all the time help is present—because the Holy Spirit is inside them ready to help them!

### The Enduement of Power on the Early Church

In the New Testament Church, it was the *exception* rather than the rule to have any believers who had *not* received the infilling of the Holy Spirit with the supernatural sign of speaking in other tongues. The apostles recognized the necessity of the indwelling Spirit of God, and they stressed this in their teachings to new converts.

**ACTS 8:14–15**
14 Now when the apostles which were at Jerusalem heard that Samaria had received the word of God, they sent unto them Peter and John:
15 Who, when they were come down, prayed for them, that they might receive the Holy Ghost.

**ACTS 9:17**
17 And Ananias went his way, and entered into the house; and putting his hands on him said, Brother Saul, the Lord, even Jesus, that appeared unto thee in the way as thou camest, hath sent me, that thou mightest receive thy sight, and be filled with the Holy Ghost.

**ACTS 19:1–2**
1 And it came to pass, that, while Apollo was at Corinth, Paul having passed through the upper coasts came to Ephesus: and finding certain disciples,
2 He said unto them, Have ye received the Holy Ghost since ye believed? And they said unto him, We have not so much as heard whether there be any Holy Ghost.

Certainly the Church today is no less in need of this enduement of power!

The Apostle Paul said, *"Know ye not that ye are the temple of God, and that the Spirit of God dwelleth in you?"* (1 Cor. 3:16).

*The Amplified* version of this verse reads, *"Do you not discern and understand that you [the whole church at*

*Corinth] are God's temple (His sanctuary), and that God's Spirit has His permanent dwelling in you [to be at home in you, collectively as a church and also individually]?"*

We are the temple of God. God indwells us not only as a Body, but as individuals.

Notice the expression, "to be at home in you." God is actually making His home in our bodies! No longer does He dwell in a man-made Holy of Holies, as in Old Testament times.

In those times, it was required that every Jewish male present himself before the Lord at least once a year in Jerusalem. The men had to travel to Jerusalem, because the presence of God was *only* in the Holy of Holies. No one except the High Priest dared approach the holy presence, and he only with great precautions. Anyone else who intruded into the holy place fell dead instantly.

But now all this has been done away with, and we may *". . . come boldly unto the throne of grace, that we may obtain mercy, and find grace to help in time of need"* (Heb. 4:16).

Just before Jesus died, He said, *"It is finished."* He was not talking about the Plan of Redemption's being finished, because it wasn't finished when He died. He had to rise from the dead and ascend into the heavenly Holy of Holies with His own blood as a sacrifice to obtain eternal redemption for us.

Then He had to ascend on high to be seated at the right hand of the Father and begin His mediatorial intercession; to be the Mediator between God and man. Until then, the New Covenant was not in effect.

No, when Jesus said on the cross, *"It is finished,"* He was referring to the Old Testament's being finished!

When this happened, the veil, or curtain, that separated the Holy of Holies was torn in two from top to bottom.

The Jewish historian Josephus tells us this curtain was 40 feet wide, 20 feet high, and 4 inches thick. Imagine how difficult it would be for a man to tear something this size in two! But notice that the Scriptures do not say the curtain was torn from the bottom to the top. Rather, *". . . the veil of the temple was rent in twain from the TOP TO THE BOTTOM . . ."* (Matt. 27:51). This signified that it was God, not man, who tore down the curtain—the barrier— separating man from God!

The presence of God moved out of that man-made Holy of Holies never to dwell there again. Now His divine presence indwells us.

To be filled with the Holy Spirit is much more than just a thrilling experience. The Holy Spirit, the divine personality, actually comes to live in you!

*". . . For ye are the temple of the living God; as God hath said, I WILL DWELL IN THEM, AND WALK IN THEM;*

*and I will be their God, and they shall be my people"* (2 Cor. 6:16).

How many of us fully realize this marvelous truth? How many of us recognize the fact that in us—ready for our use—is *all the power we will ever need to put us over in life?*

If we will begin to believe what the Bible says—to confess what God's Word says—the Holy Spirit will rise up within us and give illumination to our minds. He will give direction to our spirits, health to our bodies, and help in every aspect of life. We can be conscious of His indwelling presence every moment.

Let us look again at *The Amplified* version of First Corinthians 3:16, *". . . God's Spirit has His permanent dwelling in you [to be at home in you] . . ."*

Few of us are conscious of God's living in our bodies, for we could not be conscious of His living within us and still talk the way we do!

For example, when asked to do some difficult thing, how quick we are to say, "No, I can't do that."

Why do we do this? It is because we are trusting in ourselves to do it, and we know we don't have the ability. But if we know He is in us, we know He has the ability. We change the "I can't" to "I can," because we are trusting in Him.

We say, "I can, because He is in me. Greater is He that is in me than he that

is in the world." No matter what impossibilities we may be facing, we can say, "He will make me a success, because He indwells me."

This kind of believing—this kind of talking—is faith talking, and it will put Him to work for us.

Some people have a wrong conception of the Holy Spirit's role in their lives. They think He will come in, take over, and run the show. They expect Him to become sort of a boss, without their having to do anything.

The Holy Spirit, however, is a gentleman. He will guide and direct us; He will prompt and urge; but He never will force or control our life.

Demons and evil spirits *control* those whom they enter, forcing them to do things they don't want to do, but the Holy Spirit gently leads and guides us. He won't do anything until we put Him to work for us, because He is sent to be our Helper. He is not sent to *do* the job, but to *help* us do it.

*The Amplified* version of Ephesians 3:16–17 says, *"May he grant you out of the rich treasury of His glory to be strengthened and reinforced with mighty power in the inner man by the [Holy] Spirit [Himself indwelling your innermost being and personality]. May Christ through your faith [actually] dwell (settle down, abide, make His permanent home) in your hearts! May you be rooted deep in love and founded securely on love."*

In this passage of Scripture, Paul was writing to those who already were born again and filled with the Holy Spirit.

How does Christ abide in our hearts? Through our faith. Christ wants to dwell in our hearts; to reign as King on the throne of our hearts. But too few have allowed Him to do so.

People look outside themselves for God to do something. They sing, "Come by here, Lord. Come by here." (We think if we could only get Him to "come by here," He might do something for us!)

Then we sing, "Reach out and touch the Lord as He goes by." But this is all sense knowledge. It is all on the outside. It is all physical.

Someone might argue, "But in the Bible didn't the woman with the issue of blood reach out and touch the Lord?" Yes, but that was when He was here on the earth in physical form. Now He is not only *with* us; He is *in* us. We don't have to reach out and touch Him; He is always in us.

But this is not going to do us any good unless we know it and believe it, because the Holy Spirit will not rise up and take over. When we know He is in there, and we act intelligently on God's Word, He will work through us.

We can say, "Greater is He that is in me than he that is in the world. The Greater One is in me. I am depending on Him. He will put me over. He will make me a success, because He is in me. The Master of Creation is making His home in my body."

---

---

# Lesson 13

# The God-Kind of Faith

**Bible Texts:** Mark 11:12–14,20–24; Romans 10:13–14,17

**Central Truth:** The kind of faith that spoke the universe into existence is dealt to our hearts.

There are two things to notice about the God-kind of faith. First, a man believes with his heart. Second, he believes with his words. It isn't enough just to believe in your heart. In order to get God to work for you you must believe with your words also.

Jesus said, *"Whosoever shall say . . . and shall not doubt in his heart, but shall believe that those things which he saith shall come to pass; he shall have whatsoever he saith"* (Mark 11:23). This is the unalterable law of faith.

**MARK 11:12–14,20–24**

**12** And on the morrow, when they were come from Bethany, he was hungry:

**13** And seeing a fig tree afar off having leaves, he came, if haply he might find anything thereon: and when he came to it, he found nothing but leaves; for the time of figs was not yet.

**14** And Jesus answered and said unto it, No man eat fruit of thee hereafter for ever. And his disciples heard it. . . .

**20** And in the morning, as they passed by, they saw the fig tree dried up from the roots.

**21** And Peter calling to remembrance saith unto him, Master, behold, the fig tree which thou cursedst is withered away.

**22** And Jesus answering saith unto them, Have faith in God.

**23** For verily I say unto you, That whosoever shall say unto this mountain, Be thou removed, and be thou cast into the sea; and shall not doubt in his heart, but shall believe that those things which he saith shall come to pass; he shall have whatsoever he saith.

**24** Therefore I say unto you, What things soever ye desire, when ye pray, believe that ye receive them, and ye shall have them.

Let us focus our attention on the statement "Have faith in God," or, as the margin reads, "Have the faith of God." Greek scholars tell us this should be translated, "Have the God-kind of faith."

Jesus demonstrated that He had the God-kind of faith. While He was afar off, He saw that the fig tree had leaves. But as He approached it, looking for fruit, He saw it was barren. Some have questioned why Jesus looked for figs on this tree when it was not the season for the figs to be ripe. However, in that country, trees that retained their leaves usually also had figs.

Finding no fruit on the tree, Jesus said, *"No man eat fruit of thee hereafter for ever."*

The next day as Jesus and His disciples passed by again, they found the tree dried up from its roots. Amazed, Peter said, *"Master, behold, the fig tree which thou cursedst is withered away."*

It was then that Jesus made the statement, *"Have faith in God* [have the faith of God, or the God-kind of faith]. *For verily I say unto you, That whosoever shall say unto this mountain, Be thou removed, and be thou cast into the sea; and shall not doubt in his heart, but shall believe that those things which he saith shall come to pass; he shall have whatsoever he saith"* (vv. 22–23).

After telling His disciples in verse 22 to have the God-kind of faith, Jesus went on to explain what this meant:

The God-kind of faith is the kind of faith in which a man *believes* with his heart and *says* with his mouth that which he believes in his heart—and it comes to pass.

Jesus showed He had that kind of faith, because He *believed* what He said would come to pass. He said to the tree, *"No man eat fruit of thee hereafter for ever."*

This is the kind of faith that spoke the world into existence! *"Through faith we understand that the worlds were framed by the word of God, so that things which are seen were not made of things which do appear"* (Heb. 11:3).

How did He do it? God *believed* that what He *said* would come to pass. He spoke the Word, and there was an earth. He spoke the vegetable kingdom into existence. He spoke the animal kingdom into existence. He spoke the heavens, the moon, the sun, the stars, and the universe into existence. He said it, and it was so!

That is the God-kind of faith. God believed what He said would come to pass, and it did.

## The Measure of Faith

Jesus demonstrated the God-kind of faith to His disciples, and then He told them that they, too, had that kind of faith—the faith that a man believes with his heart, says with his mouth what he believes, and it comes to pass.

Someone might say, "I want that kind of faith. I am going to pray that God will give it to me." However, you don't need to pray for it; you already have it!

*"For I say, through the grace given unto me, to every man that is among you, not to think of himself more highly than he ought to think; but to think soberly, according as God hath dealt to every man the measure of faith"* (Rom. 12:3).

Notice that Paul wrote this to believers, because he says, *"to every man that is among you."* The epistle of Romans was not written to the sinners in the world; it is a letter to Christians, because it is addressed *"To all that be in Rome, beloved of God, called to be saints . . ."* (Rom. 1:7). And in it, Paul tells them that God has given *"to every man the measure of faith."*

Paul also said, *"For by grace are ye saved through faith; and that not of yourselves: it is the gift of God"* (Eph. 2:8). Paul is saying here that this faith is not of yourself. He is not referring to grace, because everyone knows that grace is of God.

Paul is saying that the faith by which we are saved is not of ourselves; it is not a natural, human faith. It is given to sinners by God. And how does God give the sinner faith to be saved?

Romans 10:17 says, *"So then faith cometh by hearing, and hearing by the word of God."* In these verses Paul has said faith: (1) is given, (2) is dealt, and (3) comes.

## Believing and Saying— The Keys to Faith

Notice the words of Romans 10:8, *"But what saith it? The word is nigh thee, even IN THY MOUTH, and IN THY HEART: that is, THE WORD OF FAITH, which we preach."*

How does this compare with the words of Jesus in Mark 11:23? Paul's writings to the Romans agree exactly with what Jesus told His disciples when He said, *"Whosoever shall say . . . and shall not doubt in his heart, but shall believe . . . shall have whatsoever he saith."*

We see here the basic principle inherent in the God-kind of faith: believing with the heart and saying it with the mouth. Jesus believed it, and He said it. God believed it, and He said it, speaking the earth into existence.

Verses 9 and 10 of this same 10th chapter of Romans say, *"That if thou shalt confess with thy mouth the Lord Jesus, and shalt believe in thine heart that God hath raised him from the dead, thou shalt be saved. For with the heart man believeth unto righteousness; and with the mouth confession is made unto salvation."*

A measure of faith is dealt to the sinner through hearing the Word. Then he uses it to create the reality of salvation in his own life.

When Christians are asked, "When were you saved?" they often answer by saying something like, "About nine o'clock on the night of July 10."

They are mistaken, however. God saved them nearly 2,000 years ago! It only became a reality to them when they believed it and confessed it.

Salvation belongs to everyone. Every man and woman in this world has a legal right to salvation. Jesus died for the whole world, not just for you and me. When the truth is preached to the sinner, it causes faith to come. When he believes and confesses, he creates the reality of it in his own life by his faith.

**ROMANS 10:13–14,17**
**13 For whosoever shall call upon the name of the Lord shall be saved.**
**14 How then shall they call on him in whom they have not believed? and how shall they believe in him of whom they have not heard? and how shall they hear without a preacher? . . .**
**17 So then faith cometh by hearing, and hearing by the word of God.**

Just as faith comes from hearing the Word of God, so does anything we receive from God. The God-kind of faith comes by hearing God's Word. In other words, God causes the God-kind of faith to come into the hearts of those who hear.

No wonder Jesus said, *"Take heed therefore how ye hear"* (Luke 8:18). You can't let it go in one ear and out the other, because that won't do any good. Faith won't come. If you act as if the Word of God were some fairy tale, faith will not come. But when you accept it reverently and sincerely—when you act upon it—faith comes.

Paul wrote to the Church at Corinth, *"We having the same spirit of faith, according as it is written, I believed, and therefore have I spoken; we also believe, and therefore speak"* (2 Cor. 4:13).

Paul said we have the same spirit of faith. And what belonged to the Church at Corinth belongs to the Church today. On no occasion did Paul or any of the apostles ever write to encourage the people to believe; never did they tell them to have faith.

Our having to encourage believers to believe or have faith is a result of the Word of God's having lost its reality to us. We *are* believers!

When our children are away from home, we don't have to write them and say, "Be sure to keep breathing." They will continue to breathe as long as they are alive. Neither do we have to encourage believers to believe, because that is what they are—believers.

How many of us realize that our words dominate us? *"Thou art snared with the words of thy mouth,"* we read in Proverbs 6:2. Another version says, "Thou art taken captive with the words of thy mouth."

A young man once told me he never was defeated until he confessed that he was. One Baptist minister put it this way: "You said you could not, and the moment you said it, you were defeated. You said you did not have faith, and doubt rose up like a giant and bound you. You are imprisoned with your own words. You talk failure, and failure holds you in bondage."

Defeat and failure do not belong to the child of God. *God never made a failure!* God made us new creatures. We are not born of the will of the flesh or the will of man, but of the will of God. We are created in Christ Jesus. Failures are man-made. They are made by wrong believing and wrong thinking.

First John 4:4 says, *"greater is he that is in you, than he that is in the world."* Learn to trust the Greater One who is in you. He is mightier than anything in the world.

*God created the universe with words! Words filled with faith are the most powerful things in all the world.*

The key to the God-kind of faith is *believing* with the heart and *confessing* with the mouth.

Our lips can make us millionaires or keep us paupers.

Our lips can make us victors or keep us captives.

We can fill our words with faith, or we can fill them with doubt.

We can fill our words with love that will melt the coldest heart, or we can fill them with hate and poison.

We can fill our words with love that will help the discouraged and brokenhearted; with faith that will stir heaven.

We can make our words breathe the very atmosphere of heaven.

Our faith will never rise above the words of our lips. Jesus told the woman with the issue of blood that her faith had made her whole.

Thoughts may come, and they may persist in staying. But if we refuse to put those thoughts into words, they die unborn!

Cultivate the habit of thinking big things. Learn to use words that will react upon your own spirit.

Faith's confessions create realities.

Realization follows the confession.

Confession precedes possession.

---

**Memory Text:**

"But what saith it? The word is nigh thee, even in thy mouth, and in thy heart: that is, the word of faith, which we preach."
—Rom. 10:8

---

*Why should you consider attending*

# RHEMA
# Bible Training Center?

*Here are a few good reasons:*

- Training at one of the top Spirit-filled Bible schools anywhere
- Teaching based on steadfast faith in God's Word
- Growth in your spiritual walk coupled with practical training in effective ministry
- Specialization in the area of your choosing: Youth or Children's Ministry, Evangelism, Pastoral Care, Missions, Biblical Studies, or Supportive Ministry
- Optional intensive third-year programs: School of Worship, School of Pastoral Ministry, School of World Missions, and General Extended Studies
- Worldwide ministry opportunities—while you're in school
- An established network of churches and ministries around the world who depend on RHEMA to supply full-time staff and support ministers
- A two-year evening school taught entirely in Spanish is also available. Log on to **www.cebrhema.org** for more information.

**Call today for information or application material.**
1-888-28-FAITH (1-888-283-2484)
## **www.rbtc.org**

RHEMA Bible Training Center admits students of any race, color, or ethnic origin.

# Always on.

For the latest news and information on products,
media, podcasts, study resources, and
special offers, visit us online 24 hours a day.

## Free Subscription!

Call now to receive a free subscription to *The Word of Faith* magazine from Kenneth Hagin Ministries. Receive encouragement and spiritual refreshment from . . .

- *Faith-building articles from Kenneth W. Hagin, Lynette Hagin, and others*
- *"Timeless Teaching" from the archives of Kenneth E. Hagin*
- *Feature articles on prayer and healing*
- *Testimonies of salvation, healing, and deliverance*
- *Children's activity page*
- *Updates on RHEMA Bible Training Center, RHEMA Bible Church, and other outreaches of Kenneth Hagin Ministries*

### Subscribe today for your free *Word of Faith*!

1-888-28-FAITH (1-888-283-2484)

www.rhema.org/wof

OFFER CODE—BKORD:WF

# Notes

# Notes

# Notes

# Notes

# Notes

# Notes

# Notes